COOKIES

QUICK & EASY
COOKIES

70 imaginative recipes
for the busy cook

Shirley Gill

Fenn Publishing Company Ltd

Fenn Publishing Company Ltd.
1090 Lorimar Drive
Mississauga, Ontario
Canada
L5S 1R7

ISBN: 0-919768-96-2

CREDITS

Managing Editor Samantha Gray
Art Director Jane Forster
Photographer Edward Allwright
Home Economist Valerie Eames
Typeset by Bookworm Typesetting, Manchester
Color Separation by Scantrans Pte. Ltd., Singapore
Jacket Border by Susan Williams (Home Economist)
Edward Allwright (Photographer)
Acorn Studios plc, London
(Computer Graphics)
Printed in Belgium by Proost International Book Production

METRIC CONVERSION CHART

DRY		LIQUID		
Metric	Imperial	Metric	Imperial	Cup
15 g	½ oz	30 ml	1 fl oz	
30 g	1 oz	60 ml	2 fl oz	¼ cup
60 g	2 oz	90 ml	3 fl oz	
90 g	3 oz	125 ml	4 fl oz	½ cup
125 g	4 oz	155 ml	5 fl oz	
155 g	5 oz	170 ml	5½ fl oz	⅔ cup
185 g	6 oz	185 ml	6 fl oz	
220 g	7 oz	220 ml	7 fl oz	
250 g	8 oz	250 ml	8 fl oz	1 cup
280 g	9 oz	500 ml	16 fl oz	2 cups
315 g	10 oz	600 ml	20 fl oz (1 pint)	
375 g	12 oz	750 ml	1¼ pints	
410 g	13 oz	1 litre	1¾ pints	4 cups
440 g	14 oz			
470 g	15 oz			
500 g	16 oz (1 lb)			

Contents

Introduction

Cookies, crackers, crumbles and creams – all these words conjure up pictures of one irresistible baked good.

Today supermarkets and bakeries offer a vast range of well-flavored cookies in eye-catching packages, but few can compete with the flavor, texture and aroma of the freshly baked variety. Whether you are looking for treats for parties or lunch boxes, beautifully decorated presents or simply something plain and crisp to serve with coffee, or as a dessert, you will find all the recipes you need in this book. Some recipes, like those for Florentines and shortbread, macaroons and oatcakes, have been well tested over the years. They are traditional favorites that have been handed down for generations and many variations have been added to the list.

If you are new to baking, start with the simplest, plainest recipes. When you have more experience you will find the luxurious cookies for special occasions take a little more time but are well worth the effort. This book also includes fun and colorful cookies for children both to help make and to eat, and a section on no-bake cookies, simple to make on the stovetop.

The special tips included throughout the book help you to get the best results from these recipes, and give ideas for variations, decorative finishes and effective storage.

COOKIE-MAKING EQUIPMENT

The simplest homemade cookies are easy to prepare with just basic pieces of equipment.

• Use proper measuring spoons and cups to measure ingredients accurately. Level ingredients in the spoons and cups with the back of a knife, and use a measuring jug for liquid.

• Have a strainer ready to sift dry ingredients to remove lumps and incorporate spices and leavening agents evenly.

• Use large bowls to allow room for thorough mixing, cutting in or working by hand.

• An electric mixer will save

time and effort when creaming or beating. Use a rubber spatula for folding in.

• A large rolling pin is essential for rolling out evenly. Roll out dough on a cool work surface or a marble slab, using just the minimum of flour to prevent it from sticking.

• Use a sharp knife for chopping ingredients, cutting dough cleanly and marking baked cookies into portions.

• A spatula is ideal for transferring unbaked cookies to baking sheets and baked cookies to wire racks for cooling.

• Cookies bake more evenly on flat baking sheets with low sides. Choose good-quality thick baking sheets as cheap, thin ones tend to buckle when hot.

• Cool cookies on large wire racks so that they do not overlap and bend out of shape.

• For some recipes you will also need a saucepan and heatproof bowl for melting butter, chocolate, or other ingredients; a grater; a pastry brush for glazing; and nonstick baking parchment.

If you plan to bake cookies regularly, it is worth adding the following to your collection of baking equipment:

• A pastry wheel for cutting fancy edges, and a selection of plain and shaped cookie cutters. Metal cutters are preferable as they have a sharper cutting edge than plastic ones.

• Piping equipment — large decorating bags and tips for piping soft doughs, and a selection of small bags and tips for frostings.

• Shortbread molds and a cookie press are probably the most expensive items you may want to invest in.

STORING COOKIES

• Plain unfrosted cookies keep fresh and crisp the longest. Store them in an airtight container in a cool place for up to 2 weeks.

• Richer cookies, and those that have been filled or frosted, will keep for 2 to 3 days.

Cookies with creamy fillings keep best if stored in an airtight container in the refrigerator.
- Store different types of cookies separately when possible, particularly those with strong flavors.
- Layer more delicate cookies with sheets of nonstick paper to protect them.

Freezing cookies Most rich, firm cookie doughs with a high proportion of fat freeze well for up to 3 months. Do not freeze doughs containing nuts as the flavor and texture will spoil. Either wrap and freeze whole pieces of dough, or open-freeze shaped unbaked cookies. Separate cookies can be layered with waxed paper, packed in boxes or bags and baked when required from frozen, adding a few minutes to the usual baking time.

Ready-baked cookies can also be frozen before filling or frosting. Pack delicate cookies carefully, and refresh in a hot oven before serving if wished.

COOKIE-MAKING METHODS

Cutting-in method Cookies made by this method can be plain or enriched with eggs or extra butter. Use chilled butter for cutting to prevent the flour and butter mixture from sticking together. Cut the butter into small pieces and cut it into the flour with two table knives or a pastry blender until the mixture resembles bread crumbs. Milk or eggs are usually added to bind the dough, which is then shaped or rolled out and cut as required.

Creaming method A wide variety of cookies are made by creaming, from plain orange cookies to fancy cookies and piped fingers.

Leave the butter to soften slightly by standing it in a warm place before creaming. Beat together the softened butter and sugar until it is pale, soft and creamy. After flour and any binding ingredients have been added, the dough can be kneaded lightly. If a dough that is to be rolled out is too soft, chill it in the refrigerator until firmer. Do not add extra flour or the baked cookies will be tough.

Melting method Cookies such as flapjacks, gingerbread and brandy snaps are made by this method. The butter, sugars and syrups are melted together, then the dry ingredients stirred in, often with fruit and nuts. The resulting dough is quite soft because of the high proportion of sugar, but it firms up as it cools. It can then be rolled out, spooned or pressed into baking pans.

The baked cookies crisp as they cool, so they need to be either shaped quickly or left to stand for a few minutes before removing from the baking sheets.

Beaten method This method is used for meringue and cake-like cookies, as well as for thin, crisp wafers.

The eggs and sugar are beaten together until pale and creamy, preferably with an electric mixer. Then melted butter, flour and any flavorings are beaten in, and the soft mixture is ready for spooning or piping on to greased baking sheets.

Refrigerator cookies These cookies, are usually made by the creaming method, but the dough is too soft to work with until it has been thoroughly chilled. Chilled dough can be kept in the refrigerator for up to a week before slicing and baking.

No-bake cookies Although these are not true cookies, they are just as delicious and quick to make. The method usually involves melting butter, chocolate and sugar in a saucepan and adding cereals or crushed crackers, fruit and nuts. The soft dough is then shaped or pressed into a pan and chilled for several hours until it sets into a wonderful, chewy cookie.

Arrowroot Rings

INGREDIENTS

Makes 48

1 cup all-purpose flour

1 cup arrowroot

¼ cup butter

6 tbsp sugar

1 egg yolk, beaten

¼ cup milk

1   Preheat the oven to 350°F. Lightly grease several baking sheets.

2   Sift the flour and arrowroot into a bowl. Cut in the butter until the mixture resembles fine bread crumbs. Stir the sugar into the mixture. Add the egg yolk and milk, then mix to form a stiff dough. Knead lightly.

3   Roll out the dough on a lightly floured surface to ⅛ inch thick. Using a 2½-inch fluted cutter, cut out circles from the dough. Place on the baking sheets and remove the centers with a 1-inch cutter. Prick with a fork.

4   Knead and re-roll the trimmings. Continue cutting out more rings until all the dough is used up.

5   Bake for 10 minutes or until very lightly browned. Transfer to wire racks to cool.

COOK'S TIPS
If you do not have a cutter small enough to cut out the centers of the rings, use an apple corer or the wide end of a decorating tip. If cutters stick to the dough, dip them lightly in flour.

Swiss Whirls

1   Preheat the oven to 350°F. Arrange 20 petits fours cases on baking sheets.

2   Put the butter, confectioners' sugar and vanilla extract into a bowl and beat until light and creamy.

3   Sift in the flour and cornstarch, then work in well.

4   Spoon the mixture into a decorating bag fitted with a medium star tip. Pipe whirls into the petits fours cases and decorate each whirl with pieces of angelica and cherry.

5   Bake for 15 to 18 minutes until very lightly browned. Transfer to a wire rack to cool.

6 When the cookies are cold, remove the case from each one and dredge with confectioners' sugar.

COOK'S TIP
This dough can be quite firm to pipe. It will be soft enough if you stand the butter in a warm place before starting and beat the mixture thoroughly.

INGREDIENTS

Makes 20

½ cup butter

¼ cup confectioners' sugar, sifted

few drops vanilla extract

¾ cup all-purpose flour

¼ cup cornstarch

small piece of angelica, finely chopped

candied cherry, finely chopped

confectioners' sugar for dredging

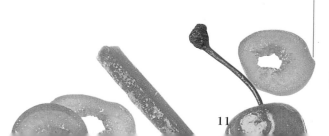

Ginger Cookies

INGREDIENTS

Makes 30

½ cup butter

1½ cups sugar

1 egg, beaten

2¼ cups self-rising flour

1½ tsp ground ginger

1   Preheat the oven to 300°F. Lightly grease several baking sheets.

2   Put the butter and sugar in a bowl and beat until light and creamy. Gradually beat in the egg.

3   Sift the flour and ginger into the mixture and work in to make a dough. Knead lightly.

4   Divide the dough into 30 pieces and roll each piece into a ball. Put on the baking sheets, spacing apart.

5   Bake for about 40 minutes until risen, hollow and crisp, and very lightly browned. Cool on wire racks.

Petticoat Tails

1   Put the butter and sugar in a bowl and beat until light and creamy.

2   Sift the flours into the mixture and work in by hand to form a soft dough.

3   Lightly flour the work surface. Divide the dough into 2 pieces and roll out each piece to fit a 7-inch round cake pan.

4   Place the dough in the pans and press in gently. Prick well with a fork and flute the edges if wished. Chill for 30 minutes. Preheat the oven to 300°F.

5   Bake the shortbread for 40 to 45 minutes until pale golden.

6   Mark each shortbread into 8 portions and dredge with sugar while hot. Cool in the tins.

COOK'S TIP
For shortbread, and other cookies with a high proportion of fat, it is preferable to use butter, rather than margarine, because of its superior flavor.

INGREDIENTS

Makes 16

1 cup butter

6 tbsp sugar

2 ¼ cups all-purpose flour

½ cup rice flour

sugar to dredge

Langues de Chat

INGREDIENTS

Makes 30

¼ cup butter

5 tbsp sugar

1 egg, beaten

½ cup all-purpose flour

1 Preheat the oven to 425°F. Lightly grease several baking sheets and line them with nonstick baking parchment.

2 Put the butter and sugar in a bowl and beat until light and creamy. Gradually beat in the egg.

3 Sift the flour into the mixture, then fold it in to make a very soft dough.

4 Spoon the dough into a decorating bag fitted with a ¼-inch plain tip. Pipe 30 x 3-inch strips onto the baking sheets, spacing them very well apart.

5 Bake for 5 minutes until the edges are lightly browned. Leave to stand for 1 minute before transferring to wire racks to cool.

Gingersnaps

1　Preheat the oven to 350°F. Lightly grease 2 baking sheets.

2　Put the butter, syrup, sugar and molasses into a saucepan and stir over gentle heat until melted. Leave to cool slightly.

3　Sift the flour, ginger, cinnamon and baking soda into a bowl. Stir into the melted ingredients until smooth.

4　Put 18 rounded teaspoons of dough onto the baking sheets, leaving room for spreading during baking. Bake for 10 to 12 minutes until browned.

5　Leave to stand for 1 minute, then transfer to wire racks to cool and harden.

INGREDIENTS

Makes 18

½ cup butter

2 ½ tbsp light corn syrup

2 tbsp light brown sugar

1 ½ tbsp light molasses

1 cup self-rising flour

1 tsp ground ginger

1 tsp ground cinnamon

½ tsp baking soda

Wheat Crackers

INGREDIENTS

Makes 20

1½ cups whole wheat flour

½ cup all-purpose flour

6 tbsp butter, chilled and diced

2 tbsp light brown sugar

1 egg, beaten

1 to 2 tsp milk

1   Preheat the oven to 400°F. Lightly grease 2 baking sheets.

2   Mix together the whole wheat and all-purpose flours. Cut in the butter until the mixture resembles fine bread crumbs. Stir in the sugar.

3   Beat in the egg and milk, then mix to form a fairly firm dough. Knead lightly. On a lightly floured surface, roll out the dough into a 12 x 10-inch rectangle.

4   Using a pastry wheel or knife, cut the dough into 2½-inch squares. Place on the baking sheets and prick with a fork. Bake for about 12 minutes until lightly browned. Transfer to wire racks and allow to cool.

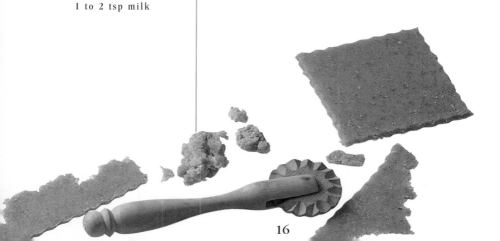

Wheat Germ Thins

1   Preheat the oven to 375°F. Lightly grease several baking sheets.

2   Mix together the flours and wheat germ in a bowl. Cut in butter until the mixture resembles fine bread crumbs. Stir in the sugar, add the egg yolk and milk and mix to make a soft dough. Knead gently.

3   On a lightly floured surface, roll out the dough ⅛ inch thick. Cut out circles with a 2½-inch fluted cutter. Place on the baking sheets. Knead and re-roll the trimmings to cut out more circles until all the dough is used up.

4   Mix together the remaining wheat germ and brown sugar to make the topping. Sprinkle over half of each circle. Bake for 7 to 8 minutes until very lightly browned, then transfer to a wire rack to cool. Dredge the other half of each biscuit with confectioners' sugar.

INGREDIENTS

Makes 30

½ cup whole wheat flour

½ cup all-purpose flour, sifted

1 tbsp wheat germ

¼ cup butter, chilled and diced

¼ cup light brown sugar

1 egg yolk, beaten

1 tbsp milk

confectioners' sugar to dredge

For the topping

2 tbsp wheat germ

4 tsp soft light brown sugar

Madeleines

INGREDIENTS

Makes 30

2 eggs, separated

½ cup sugar

½ cup unsalted
butter, melted

1 cup self-rising flour,
sifted

finely grated zest of
½ lemon

confectioners' sugar to
dredge

1   Preheat the oven to 375°F. Lightly grease and flour 30 molds on madeleine trays.

2   Put the egg yolks and sugar in a bowl and beat together until pale and creamy. Gradually beat in the butter and flour.

3   Beat the egg whites lightly with a fork, then beat into the batter, along with the lemon zest.

4   Three-quarters fill each madeleine mold with batter and smooth the tops. Bake for 12 to 15 minutes until lightly browned.

5   Transfer to wire racks to cool, then dredge with confectioners' sugar.

COOK'S TIP

These are traditionally baked in special shell-shaped molds. If you can not find a madeleine tray, use lightly greased tartlet pans.

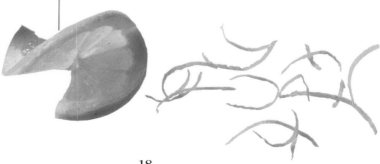

Cinnamon Snaps

1 Preheat the oven to 350°F. Lightly grease several baking sheets.

2 Put the butter and sugar in a bowl and beat until light and creamy.

3 Sift the flour and cinnamon into the bowl and work together to make a soft dough. Knead gently.

4 On a lightly floured surface, roll out the dough ⅛ inch thick.

5 Cut out circles with a 2-inch plain cutter and place on the baking sheets, spacing well apart. Knead and re-roll trimmings to cut out more circles until all the dough is used up.

6 Dredge the biscuits with sugar and bake for 8 to 9 minutes until just firm to the touch.

7 Leave the cookies to stand for a few minutes on the baking sheets, then transfer to wire racks and leave to cool.

COOK'S TIP
These cookies are soft when hot. Leave to cool slightly before removing from the baking sheets to prevent them from bending when handled and cooling into odd shapes.

INGREDIENTS

Makes 30

¼ cup butter

¼ cup sugar

½ cup all-purpose flour

1 tsp ground cinnamon

sugar to dredge

Nut and Raisin Oatcakes

INGREDIENTS

Makes 12

¾ cup all-purpose flour

1 tsp baking powder

¼ cup butter, chilled and diced

1 cup rolled oats

¾ cup mixed nuts and raisins, chopped

2 tbsp milk

1 Preheat the oven to 350°F. Lightly grease 2 baking sheets.

2 Sift the flour and baking powder into a bowl. Cut in the butter until the mixture resembles fine bread crumbs.

3 Stir the oats and nuts and raisins in. Add the milk and mix to make a firm dough. Knead gently.

4 On a lightly floured surface, roll out the dough to ¼ inch thick. Cut out circles with a 2¼-inch fluted cutter. Place on the baking sheets. Knead and re-roll the trimmings. Continue cutting out more circles until all the dough is used up.

5 Bake for about 12 minutes until very lightly browned. Transfer to a wire rack to cool.

COOK'S TIP
Buy a package of ready-mixed nuts and raisins, including almonds, hazelnuts and peanuts, to get the best variety.

Lemon and Lime Thins

1   Preheat the oven to 350°F. Lightly grease several baking sheets.

2   Finely grate the zest from the lemons and limes. Reserve a little for decorating cookies with.

3   Put the butter, sugar and grated zest in a bowl and beat until light and creamy. Beat in the egg yolk.

4   Sift in the flour and mix to make a smooth dough. Knead lightly.

5   On a lightly floured surface, roll out the dough to ⅛ inch thick.

6   Cut out circles with a 2-inch cutter and place on the baking sheets. Knead and re-roll trimmings to cut out more circles until all the dough is used up.

7   Bake for 8 to 9 minutes until very lightly browned, then transfer to wire racks to cool.

8   Sprinkle the cookies with reserved lemon and lime zest and dredge with confectioners' sugar.

INGREDIENTS

Makes 60

2 lemons

2 limes

½ cup butter

6 tbsp sugar

1 egg yolk, beaten

1¼ cups self-rising flour

confectioners' sugar to dredge

Fruity Flapjacks

INGREDIENTS

Makes 16

½ cup butter

½ cup lightly packed light brown sugar

2½ tbsp light corn syrup

2½ cups oatmeal

½ cup currants

½ cup pitted dates, chopped

⅓ cup candied cherries, chopped

1   Preheat the oven to 375°F. Lightly grease an 11 x 7-inch baking pan.

2   Put the butter, sugar and syrup into a pan and stir over low heat until melted.

3   Stir in the oatmeal, currants, dates and cherries. Spoon dough into the pan, pressing down well. Bake for 20 to 25 minutes until lightly browned.

4   Leave to cool for 5 minutes, then mark into 16 fingers, cutting into 4 lengthwise and 4 widthwise. Leave to cool in the pan.

Sesame and Sunflower Bars

1   Preheat the oven to 350°F. Lightly grease a 7-inch square baking pan and line it with nonstick baking parchment.

2   Put the butter, sugar, corn syrup and honey into a saucepan and stir over low heat until melted. Stir in the oatmeal and seeds.

3   Spoon the mixture into the baking pan, pressing down well. Bake for about 30 minutes or until browned and firm to touch.

4   Leave to cool for a few minutes, then mark into 14 bars by dividing the square in half and cutting each into 7 pieces. Leave to cool in the pan.

VARIATION

Replace the sunflower seeds with pumpkin seeds and a few chopped nuts.

INGREDIENTS

Makes 14

½ cup butter

6 tbsp light brown sugar

3 tbsp light corn syrup

½ tbsp honey

1 cup oatmeal

2 tbsp sunflower seeds

1 tbsp sesame seeds

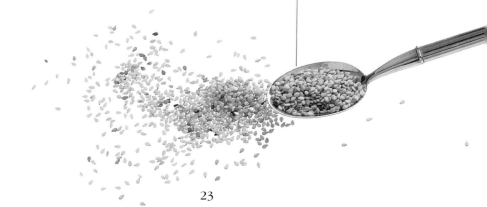

Orange Cookies

INGREDIENTS

Makes 30

½ cup butter

¾ cup sugar

1 egg yolk, beaten

grated zest of ½ orange

2 cups all-purpose flour

2 tbsp orange juice

½ cup confectioners'
sugar, sifted

1 tbsp orange juice

grated zest of ½ orange

1   Lightly grease several baking sheets.

2   Put the butter and sugar in a bowl and beat until light and creamy. Beat in the egg yolk and orange zest.

3   Sift the flour into the bowl and stir in the orange juice. Mix to make a fairly firm dough.

4   Knead the dough lightly. On a lightly floured surface, roll out the dough ¼ inch thick.

5   Cut out circles with a 2½-inch fluted cutter and place on the baking sheets. Knead and re-roll trimmings to cut out more circles until all the dough is used up. Chill for 30 minutes. Meanwhile, preheat the oven to 350°F.

6   Bake the cookies for 15 to 20 minutes until lightly browned. Transfer to wire racks to cool.

7   Meanwhile, make the topping. Beat together the confectioners' sugar, orange juice and orange rind. Drizzle or spread the icing over the biscuits and leave to set.

Almond Macaroons

1   Preheat the oven to 350°F. Line 2 or 3 baking sheets with rice paper.

2   Put the egg whites in a clean, grease-free bowl. Beat until stiff but not dry. Gently fold in the sugar, ground almonds and almond extract.

3   Spoon the dough into a decorating bag fitted with a ½-inch round tip. Pipe 28 small mounds onto the baking sheets, spacing well apart. Top with halved almonds.

4   Bake for 20 minutes until lightly browned. Leave to cool on the baking sheets.

5   Remove the cold macaroons, tearing away excess rice paper.

INGREDIENTS

Makes 28

rice paper

2 egg whites

¾ cup + 2 tbsp sugar

1 ½ cups finely ground blanched almonds

few drops almond extract

14 blanched almonds, halved

Pecan and Raisin Cookies

INGREDIENTS

Makes 24

10 tbsp butter

6 tbsp light brown sugar

¼ cup sugar

1 egg, beaten

few drops vanilla extract

1 ½ cups all-purpose flour

½ tsp baking soda

½ cup pecan nuts,
chopped

⅓ cup raisins

1 Preheat the oven to 350°F. Lightly grease several baking sheets.

2 Put the butter and sugars in a bowl and beat until light and creamy. Beat in the egg and vanilla extract.

3 Sift the flour and baking soda into the bowl. Stir in thoroughly, along with the pecan nuts and raisins.

4 Put 24 heaped teaspoonfuls of the dough onto the baking sheets, spacing well apart.

5 Bake for 15 minutes until lightly browned. Leave to stand for 1 minute before transferring to a wire rack to cool.

Chocolate-Coconut Macaroons

1 Preheat the oven to 325°F. Line 2 or 3 baking sheets with nonstick baking parchment.

2 Put the whole egg and the egg white in a bowl and beat until soft and light.

3 Gradually beat in the sugar. Beat in the cocoa, then fold in the coconut.

4 Place 24 heaped teaspoonfuls of the dough onto the baking sheets, spacing them well apart. Top with chocolate chips, if liked.

5 Bake for 20 minutes or until just firm to the touch. Leave to stand for a few minutes before transferring to wire racks to cool.

INGREDIENTS

Makes 24

1 egg

1 egg white

½ cup sugar

2 tbsp unsweetened cocoa powder, sifted

2 cups shredded coconut

chocolate chips to top (optional)

Peanut Butter Cookies

INGREDIENTS

Makes 20

6 tbsp butter

5 tbsp crunchy peanut butter

5 tbsp light brown sugar

¼ cup sugar

1 egg, beaten

1¼ cups self-rising flour

1 Preheat the oven to 350°F. Lightly grease 2 or 3 baking sheets.

2 Put the butter, peanut butter and sugars into a bowl and beat until soft and creamy. Beat in the egg.

3 Sift in the flour and stir in thoroughly. Put 20 heaped teaspoonfuls of the dough onto the baking sheets, spacing them well apart.

4 Bake for 15 to 20 minutes until slightly risen and browned. Transfer to a wire rack to cool.

Apricot Squares

1   Lightly grease 2 or 3 baking sheets. Sift the flour into a bowl. Cut in the butter until the mixture resembles coarse bread crumbs.

2   Sift in the confectioners' sugar. Stir in the egg yolk, milk and vanilla extract and mix well to form a soft dough. Knead lightly.

3   Divide the dough into 2 pieces. On a lightly floured surface, roll out each piece to an 11 x 9-inch rectangle.

4   Arrange the apricots over one rectangle and lay the second rectangle on top. Press down gently with a rolling pin to make the rectangle larger.

5   Cut into pieces about 2 inches square and place on the baking sheets.

6   Lightly score the apricot squares with a knife and chill for 30 minutes. Meanwhile, preheat the oven to 400°F.

7   Bake the squares for 15 minutes or until very lightly browned. Transfer to wire racks to cool. Dredge with confectioners' sugar.

INGREDIENTS

Makes 30

2 cups all-purpose flour

½ cup butter, chilled and diced

¾ cup confectioners' sugar

1 egg yolk, beaten

2 tbsp milk

few drops vanilla extract

1 cup ready-to-eat dried apricots, very finely chopped

confectioners' sugar for dredging

Peanut and Syrup Cookies

INGREDIENTS

Makes 20

6 tbsp butter

¼ cup light brown sugar

1 egg yolk, beaten

1 cup self-rising flour

For the topping

1 tsp light corn syrup

½ tsp honey

1 tbsp skinned peanuts,
chopped

1 Preheat the oven to 375°F. Lightly grease 2 or 3 baking sheets.

2 Put the butter and sugar in a bowl and beat until light and creamy. Beat in the egg yolk.

3 Sift in the flour and mix in to make a smooth dough. Knead gently.

4 On a lightly floured surface, roll out the dough ⅛ inch thick. Cut out 2-inch shapes and place on baking sheets. Knead and re-roll the trimmings to cut out more shapes until all the dough is used up.

5 In a small bowl, mix together warmed syrup and honey. Drizzle syrup in the center of the cookies and sprinkle with the chopped peanuts.

6 Bake for about 8 minutes until golden brown. Transfer to a wire rack to cool.

COOK'S TIP
These cookies are best eaten within 2 or 3 days as they lose their crispness.

Golden Raisin Wedges

1 Preheat the oven to 375°F. Lightly grease 2 or 3 baking sheets.

2 Put the butter and sugar in a bowl and beat until light and creamy. Beat in the egg yolk.

3 In another bowl, sift together the flour, apple pie spice and baking soda. Add to the mixture, together with the sour cream and golden raisins. Mix thoroughly to form a soft dough.

4 Divide the dough into 4 pieces. On a lightly floured surface, roll out each piece of dough into a 6-inch circle.

5 Cut each circle into 6 wedges and place on baking sheets.

6 Bake for 16 to 18 minutes until lightly browned. Transfer to a wire rack to cool.

INGREDIENTS

Makes 24

½ cup butter

⅔ cup light brown sugar

1 egg yolk, beaten

2 cups self-rising flour

½ tsp apple pie spice

¼ tsp baking soda

¼ cup sour cream

½ cup seedless golden raisins

New Zealand Cookies

MADE '95
5ml scoops

INGREDIENTS

Heat
_ow_
sypie

Makes 20

5 tbsp butter

2 tsp light corn syrup

1 tsp honey

¼ tsp baking soda

6 tbsp sugar

½ cup all-purpose flour,
sifted

⅔ cup quick-cooking
oatmeal

½ cup shredded coconut

1   Preheat the oven to 300°F. Lightly grease 2 or 3 baking sheets.

2   Put the butter, syrup and honey into a saucepan and stir over low heat until melted.

3   Dissolve the baking soda in 1 tbsp of water. Stir into the melted mixture. Stir in the sugar, flour, oatmeal and coconut and mix thoroughly.

4   Put 20 teaspoonfuls of the dough onto the baking sheets, spacing them well apart. Bake for 20 minutes until golden. Transfer to wire racks to cool.

(THEY
SPREAD)

Hazelnut and Honey Bows

1   Put the butter and honey in a bowl and beat until light and creamy. Sift in the flour, then add the ground hazelnuts and stir together to form a soft dough.

2   On a lightly floured surface, knead the dough, then shape into a 6-inch-long roll. Wrap the dough in waxed paper and chill for 3 to 4 hours.

3   Meanwhile, preheat the oven to 350°F. Lightly grease several baking sheets.

4   Cut the chilled dough into ⅛-inch-thick slices. Cut each slice in half and press the rounded ends together to form a bow.

5   Place the bows on the baking sheets and press a hazelnut in the center of each one.

6   Bake for 8 minutes until lightly browned. Leave to stand for 1 minute before transferring to a wire rack to cool.

INGREDIENTS

Makes 36

6 tbsp butter

¼ cup honey

1 ¼ cups all-purpose flour

1 cup finely ground
toasted, skinned hazelnuts

36 whole blanched
hazelnuts

Mint Chocolate Cookies

INGREDIENTS

Makes 40

½ cup + 2 tbsp butter

¾ cups confectioners'
sugar, sifted

1 egg yolk, beaten

3 oz semisweet chocolate

2 tbsp milk

1¾ cups self-rising flour

4 oz mint-flavored
chocolate sticks

1   Put the butter and sugar in a bowl and beat until light and creamy. Beat in the egg yolk.

2   Break up the chocolate and put in a small pan with the milk. Stir over very low heat until melted.

3   Sift the flour into the butter mixture, then add the chocolate and milk and work together to form a very soft dough.

4   Lightly flour a large piece of waxed paper. Turn out the dough onto the paper and, using a spatula, shape into a roll about 10 inches long. Wrap up the roll and chill for 4 to 5 hours.

5   Meanwhile, preheat the oven to 375°F. Lightly grease several baking sheets.

6   Cut the chilled dough into 40 x ¼-inch-thick slices. Place on the baking sheets.

7   Bake for 10 to 12 minutes until just firm to the touch. Leave to stand for a few minutes, then transfer to wire racks to cool.

8   To decorate, melt the mint chocolate sticks in a bowl over a pan of hot water. Drizzle over the cookies and leave to set.

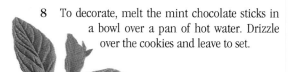

Coffee Jumbles

1 Put the butter and sugar in a bowl and beat until light and creamy. Beat in the egg yolk.

2 Dissolve the coffee granules in 2 tsp warm water.

3 Sift the flour into the creamed mixture and mix in with the dissolved coffee to make a soft dough.

4 On a lightly floured surface, knead lightly to blend in the coffee thoroughly. Wrap the dough in waxed paper and chill for at least 30 minutes. Lightly grease 2 or 3 baking sheets.

5 When required, cut off small pieces of dough and roll in sugar into thin strips 6 inches long. Twist into "S" shapes and place on the baking sheets. Chill for 30 minutes. Meanwhile, preheat the oven to 350°F.

6 Bake for 12 to 15 minutes until just firm to the touch. Transfer to a wire rack to cool.

INGREDIENTS

Makes 26

½ cup butter

½ cup sugar

1 egg yolk, beaten

1 tbsp instant coffee granules

2 cups all-purpose flour

a little extra sugar for rolling

Chocolate Cherry Slices

INGREDIENTS

Makes 40

½ cup + 2 tbsp butter

¾ cup sugar

1 egg yolk, beaten

1 ¾ cups all-purpose flour

⅓ cup unsweetened cocoa powder

1 tbsp milk

⅔ cup candied cherries

1   Put the butter and sugar in a bowl and beat until light and creamy. Beat in the egg yolk.

2   Sift in the flour and cocoa, then add the milk and work together to form a soft dough.

3   Turn out the dough on to a lightly floured surface and knead gently, incorporating the candied cherries. Shape into a roll about 10 inches long. Wrap in waxed paper and chill for 3 to 4 hours.

4   Meanwhile, preheat the oven to 375°F. Lightly grease several baking sheets.

5   Cut the chilled dough into ¼-inch-thick slices. Place on the baking sheets. Bake for 8 minutes until just firm to the touch. Transfer to wire racks to cool.

COOK'S TIP
Wrapped refrigerator cookie doughs can be kept chilled for up to a week. Slice off or shape and bake cookies as you need them.

Marbled Butter Cookies

1   Prepare each dough separately. For each put the butter and sugar in a bowl and beat until light and creamy. Then sift in the flour, adding the milk or egg yolk and work together.

2   Turn out each dough onto a lightly floured surface and knead gently. Flatten out slightly, then lay one piece on top of the other. Fold together to make a marbled effect.

3   Shape the dough into a roll about 10 inches long. Wrap in waxed paper and chill for 3 to 4 hours.

4   Meanwhile, preheat the oven to 375°F. Lightly grease several baking sheets.

5   Cut the chilled dough into 40 x ¼-inch-thick slices. Place on the baking sheets.

6   Bake for 8 minutes or until very lightly browned. Transfer carefully to wire racks to cool.

INGREDIENTS

Makes 40

For the light dough

5 tbsp butter

5 tbsp sugar

1 cup self-rising flour

2 tsp milk or one egg yolk

For the dark dough

5 tbsp butter

⅓ cup dark brown sugar

1 cup self-rising flour

1 egg yolk, beaten

Orange and Lemon Buttons

INGREDIENTS

Makes 32

½ cup butter

6 tbsp sugar

¾ cup self-rising flour

⅔ cup quick-cooking
oatmeal, plus 2 tbsp for
coating

¾ cup confectioners'
sugar

1 tsp orange juice
1 tsp lemon juice

few drops of orange and
yellow food coloring

small orange and yellow
candies

1　Preheat the oven to 375°F. Lightly grease 2 or 3 baking sheets.

2　Put the butter and sugar in a bowl and beat until light and creamy. Sift the flour into the bowl, then add the oatmeal and mix well to form a fairly soft dough.

3　Using lightly floured hands, roll the dough into 32 small balls, each about the size of an unshelled hazelnut. Roll in extra oats and place on the baking sheets.

4　Bake for 10 minutes or until golden. Transfer to wire racks to cool.

5　To decorate, divide the confectioners' sugar between 2 bowls. Stir orange juice and orange coloring into one bowl, and lemon juice and yellow coloring into the other.

6　Spoon a little frosting onto each button and top each with a candy. Leave to set.

Malted Milk Shapes

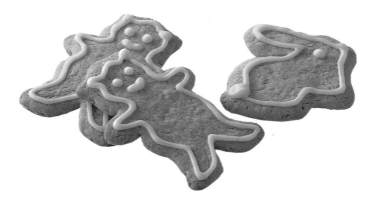

1   Preheat the oven to 375°F. Lightly grease 2 baking sheets.

2   Put the butter and sugar in a bowl and beat until light and creamy. Gradually beat in the egg, syrup and honey.

3   Sift in the flour. Add the malted milk powder and oatmeal and mix well to make a soft dough. Knead lightly.

4   On a lightly floured surface, roll out the dough ⅙ inch thick. Cut out animals with 3-inch cutters and place on the baking sheets. Knead and re-roll the trimmings to cut out more animals until all the dough is used up.

5   Bake for 7 to 8 minutes until browned. Transfer to wire racks.

6   Meanwhile, make the topping. Blend the confectioners' sugar with water until smooth and thick. Color with a few drops of food coloring if wished. Use to decorate the cookies, then leave them to dry.

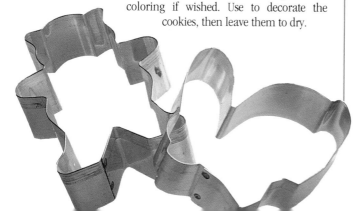

INGREDIENTS

Makes 30

6 tbsp butter

½ cup sugar

1 egg, beaten

1 ½ tbsp light corn syrup

½ tbsp honey

1 ¾ cups self-rising flour

½ cup malted milk powder

⅔ cup quick-cooking oatmeal

For the topping

½ cup confectioners' sugar, sifted

about 1 ½ tsp warm water

food coloring

Neapolitan Slices

INGREDIENTS

Makes 24

6 tbsp butter

½ cup sugar

1 cup all-purpose flour,
plus an extra 2 tbsp

few drops vanilla extract

few drops pink food
coloring

1 tbsp sweetened cocoa
powder

a little beaten egg white

1   Put the butter and sugar in a bowl and beat until light and creamy. Sift in 1 cup flour and work in to form a soft dough. Turn out the dough on to a floured surface and divide into 3 equal pieces.

2   Knead the vanilla extract and 1 tbsp flour into one piece. Knead the coloring and 1 tbsp flour into the second piece. Knead the sweetened cocoa powder into the third piece.

3   Roll out each piece of dough into a 4 x 3-inch rectangle. Place the rectangles on top of each other, brushing between the layers with egg white.

4   Wrap the dough in waxed paper and chill for at least 30 minutes. Meanwhile, preheat the oven to 350°F and grease 2 baking sheets.

5   Cut the dough into ⅓-inch-thick slices, then cut each slice in half. Place on the baking sheets.

6   Bake for 15 to 18 minutes until lightly browned. Transfer to wire racks to cool.

Raspberry and Coconut Splits

1   Preheat the oven to 350°F. Lightly grease 2 baking sheets.

2   Put the butter and sugar in a bowl and beat until light and creamy. Beat in the egg yolk.

3   Sift in the flour, add the coconut, and mix together to make a firm dough. Knead lightly on a floured surface and divide into two equal pieces.

4   Shape each piece into an 8-inch roll. Place on the baking sheets. Using a knife handle, make an indentation along the center of each roll. Fill with the jam. Sprinkle with coconut.

5   Bake for 20 minutes until golden brown. Leave to stand for a few minutes, then cut into 12 splits. Transfer to a wire rack to cool.

INGREDIENTS

Makes 12

¼ cup butter

¼ cup sugar

1 egg yolk, beaten

1 cup self-rising flour

4 tbsp shredded coconut

2 tbsp raspberry jam

a little extra shredded coconut

Cornflake Munchies

INGREDIENTS

Makes 24

¾ cup butter

½ cup light brown sugar

1 egg, beaten

1 ½ cups self-rising flour

3 tbsp unsweetened cocoa powder

2 cups cornflakes, lightly crushed

½ cup raisins

1   Preheat the oven to 350°F. Lightly grease 2 or 3 baking sheets.

2   Put the butter and sugar in a bowl and beat until light and creamy. Gradually beat in the egg.

3   Sift the flour and cocoa into the bowl, add the cornflakes and raisins and mix together thoroughly. Place 24 heaped teaspoonfuls of the mixture onto the baking sheets.

4   Bake for 15 to 18 minutes until just firm to the touch. Transfer to a wire rack to cool.

Hoops and Sticks

1   Lightly grease 2 baking sheets.

2   Put the butter and sugar in a bowl and beat until light and creamy. Beat in the egg yolk. Sift flour into the bowl and mix in.

3   Divide the mixture into 2 pieces and add cocoa to one.

4   Add a little milk to each and mix in to make smooth doughs. Knead gently.

5   Divide the plain and chocolate doughs into 10 pieces each. On a floured surface roll each piece into a thick strand 7 inches long.

6   Twist the plain and chocolate strands together and form 5 twists into hoops. Place the hoops and sticks on the baking sheets and chill for 30 minutes. Meanwhile, preheat the oven to 350°F.

7   Bake for 12 to 15 minutes until very lightly browned. Transfer to a wire rack to cool.

INGREDIENTS

Makes 10

¼ cup butter

¼ cup sugar

1 egg yolk, beaten

1 ¼ cups all-purpose flour

2 tsp unsweetened cocoa powder, sifted

1 ½ tbsp milk

Jumbo Choc-Chip Cookies

INGREDIENTS

Makes 8

½ cup butter

6 tbsp light brown sugar

¼ cup sugar

1 egg, beaten

1 ½ cups self-rising flour

⅓ cup milk chocolate pieces

⅓ cup white chocolate pieces

1 Preheat the oven to 350°F. Lightly grease several baking sheets.

2 Put the butter and sugars in a bowl and beat until light and creamy. Gradually beat in the egg.

3 Sift in the flour and stir into the mixture with the milk and white chocolate pieces.

4 Place 8 heaped tablespoonfuls of dough onto baking sheets, spacing them very well apart. Shape into circles and flatten slightly.

5 Bake for 20 to 25 minutes until browned. Leave to stand for a few minutes before transferring to a wire rack to cool.

COOK'S TIP

Allow plenty of space on the baking sheet between these cookies as they spread a lot while baking.

Gingerbread Snakes

1   Preheat the oven to 325°F. Lightly grease 2 or 3 baking sheets.

2   Put the sugar, butter, corn syrup, and honey into a pan. Stir over low heat until melted. Cool slightly.

3   Sift together the flour, ginger and baking soda. Mix into the melted ingredients with the egg to form a smooth dough.

4   Turn out the dough onto a floured surface and knead lightly. Roll out to about ¼ inch thick. Using a sharp knife, cut out snake shapes 5 to 6 inches long. Place on baking sheets and score markings on the snakes.

5   Knead and re-roll trimmings. Cut out more snakes.

6   Bake for 15 minutes until just firm to the touch. Leave to stand for a few minutes before transferring to a wire rack to cool.

7   To decorate, blend the confectioners' sugar with about 4 tsp warm water, adding food coloring if wished. Pipe onto the snakes and top with candies. Leave to set.

COOK'S TIP
This dough is also ideal for making gingerbread people, animals or fancy shapes.

INGREDIENTS

Makes 10 to 12

⅓ cup light brown sugar

¼ cup butter

2½ tbsp light corn syrup

½ tbsp honey

2 cups all-purpose flour

1 tsp ground ginger

¼ tsp baking soda

½ egg, beaten

1¼ cups confectioners' sugar, sifted, food coloring, colored candies

Golden Honey Treats

INGREDIENTS

Makes 30

½ cup butter

⅓ cup spun honey

1 egg yolk, beaten

2 cups all-purpose flour

milk to glaze

For the topping

1 oz milk chocolate

1 tbsp honey

1 tbsp confectioners'
sugar, sifted

1   Preheat the oven to 375°F. Lightly grease 2 or 3 baking sheets.

2   Put the butter and honey in a bowl and beat until light and creamy. Beat in the egg yolk.

3   Sift in the flour and work in well to make a smooth dough. Knead gently.

4   Divide the dough into 30 pieces and roll each piece into a ball. Place on the baking sheets. Mark each ball with a knife and brush with milk.

5   Bake for 10 to 12 minutes until golden brown. Transfer to wire racks to cool.

6   To make the topping, melt together the chocolate and honey in a small bowl placed over a pan of hot water. Beat in the confectioners' sugar and leave until thick enough to pipe.

7   Spoon the topping into a decorating bag fitted with a fine round tip. Pipe lines onto the cookies and leave to set.

Honey and Ginger Rings

1   Preheat the oven to 350°F. Lightly grease several baking sheets.

2   Put the sugar and butter in a bowl and beat until light and creamy.

3   In another bowl, sift together the flour, ginger, and baking soda. Add to the creamed mixture and mix in with the milk to make a smooth dough. Knead lightly.

4   On a lightly floured surface, roll out the dough to ⅛ inch thick. Cut out circles with a 2-inch cutter. Place on the baking sheets, then remove the centers with a ¾-inch cutter.

5   Knead and re-roll the trimmings to cut out more rings until all the dough is used up.

6   Bake for 7 to 8 minutes until lightly browned, then transfer to wire racks to cool.

7   Meanwhile, make the filling. Put the butter, honey, sifted confectioners' sugar and ginger in a bowl and beat until light and creamy.

8   Sandwich the rings together with the filling and store in a cool place.

INGREDIENTS

Makes about 44

⅔ cup light brown sugar

½ cup butter

2 cups self-rising flour

2 tsp ground ginger

1½ tsp baking soda

2 tbsp milk

For the filling

6 tbsp butter

¼ cup spun honey

¾ cup confectioners' sugar

¼ cup candied ginger, finely chopped

Cardamom and Lemon Wafers

INGREDIENTS

Makes 18

¼ cup butter

5 tbsp sugar

1 egg, beaten

½ cup all-purpose flour

1¼ tsp ground cardamom

confectioners' sugar to
dredge

For the filling

1 cup confectioners'
sugar, sifted

3 tbsp butter

juice and finely grated
zest of ¼ lemon

1   Preheat the oven to 375°F. Line several baking sheets with nonstick baking parchment.

2   Put the butter and sugar in a bowl and beat until light and creamy. Gradually beat in the egg. In another bowl, sift together the flour and cardamom, then fold into the butter mixture.

3   Drop 36 small teaspoonfuls of the mixture onto the baking sheets and spread into 2-inch circles.

4   Bake for 5 to 7 minutes until edges are lightly browned. Leave to stand for 1 minute before transferring to wire racks to cool.

5   Meanwhile, make the filling. Put the confectioners' sugar, butter, lemon juice and zest in a bowl. Beat until light and creamy.

6   Sandwich the cooled cookies together, dredge with confectioners' sugar and keep in a cool place.

Dark Chocolate Delights

1 Preheat the oven to 350°F. Lightly grease several baking sheets.

2 Put the butter and sifted sugar in a bowl and beat until light and creamy. Gradually beat in the egg.

3 Sift together the flour, cocoa powder and baking powder. Add to mixture and work in to make a smooth dough. Knead lightly.

4 On a lightly floured surface, roll out the dough to ⅛ inch thick. Cut out strips 1¼ inches wide, then cut each strip diagonally to make diamond shapes. Place on the baking sheets. Knead and re-roll trimmings to cut out more diamonds.

5 Bake for 7 to 8 minutes until just firm to touch, then transfer to wire racks to cool.

6 Meanwhile, make the filling. Melt the chocolate in a bowl placed over a pan of hot water. Remove from the heat, add the sifted sugar, butter and milk, then beat until light and creamy. Sandwich the diamonds together.

7 To finish, melt the remaining chocolate. Dip the top of each cookie into melted chocolate to coat. Leave in a cool place to set.

INGREDIENTS

Makes 40

½ cup butter

¾ cup confectioners' sugar

1 egg, beaten

1¾ cups all-purpose flour

⅓ cup cocoa powder

½ tsp baking powder

6 oz semisweet chocolate

For the filling

1½ oz semisweet chocolate

¾ cup confectioners' sugar

3 tbsp butter
2 tsp milk

Yogurt Crunch Creams

INGREDIENTS

Makes 20

6 tbsp butter

6 tbsp light brown sugar

1 egg yolk, beaten

1 cup + 1 tbsp self-rising flour

⅓ cup chopped toasted hazelnuts

⅓ cup quick-cooking oatmeal

For the filling

1 ½ cups confectioners' sugar, sifted

6 tbsp butter

3 tbsp plain yogurt

1   Preheat the oven to 350°F. Lightly grease several baking sheets.

2   Put the butter and sugar in a bowl and beat until light and creamy. Beat in the egg yolk.

3   Sift in the flour, add the nuts and oatmeal and mix into the creamed mixture to make a firm dough. Knead lightly.

4   On a floured surface, roll out the dough to ⅙ inch thick. Cut out circles with a 2-inch cutter. Place on the baking sheets and remove the centers from half the circles with a ¾-inch cutter. Knead and re-roll trimmings to cut out more circles and rings until all the dough is used up.

5   Bake for 6 to 7 minutes until lightly browned, then transfer to wire racks to cool.

6   Meanwhile, make the filling. Put the sugar, butter and plain yogurt in a bowl and beat until light and creamy.

7   Spread the filling on the cookie circles and top with rings. Store in a cool place.

Fudgy Mocha Fingers

1 Preheat the oven to 350°F. Lightly grease several baking sheets.

2 Dissolve the coffee granules in the water. Put the butter and sugar in a bowl and beat, then beat in the egg yolk and coffee.

3 Sift together the flour and cornstarch. Add to the creamed mixture and mix in thoroughly to make a smooth dough.

4 Knead the dough lightly to ensure the coffee blends in. On a floured surface, roll out the dough to ⅛ inch thick. Cut out fingers about 2¼ x 1-inch in size and place on the baking sheets. Knead and re-roll the trimmings to cut out more fingers.

5 Bake for 6 to 7 minutes until lightly browned, then transfer to wire racks to cool.

6 Meanwhile, make the filling. Put the coffee and water in a bowl placed over a pan of hot water. Stir to dissolve. Add the chocolate-coated fudge to the bowl. Stir until just soft.

7 Remove the bowl from the heat and beat in the cream until the filling is smooth and slightly thick. Chill until firm enough to sandwich cookies together. Dredge with confectioners' sugar.

INGREDIENTS

Makes 42

1 tbsp instant coffee granules

1 tbsp warm water

6 tbsp butter

6 tbsp sugar

1 egg yolk, beaten

1½ cups all-purpose flour

¼ cup cornstarch

For the filling

2 tsp coffee granules

1 tsp warm water

4 oz chocolate-coated fudge

2½ tbsp heavy cream

Custard Creams

INGREDIENTS

Makes 32

½ cup butter

½ cup sugar

1 egg yolk, beaten

1¾ cups all-purpose flour

⅓ cup cornstarch

1 tbsp milk

1 tbsp cornstarch

6 tbsp milk

¼ cup butter

⅓ cup confectioners' sugar

1 egg yolk, beaten

1 tbsp light cream

1   Preheat the oven to 350°F. Lightly grease several baking sheets.

2   Put the butter and sugar in a bowl and beat until light and creamy. Beat in the egg yolk.

3   Sift together the flour and cornstarch. Add to the beaten mixture and mix in thoroughly with the milk to make a smooth dough. Knead gently.

4   On a floured surface, roll out the dough to a 12-inch square.

5   Using a pastry wheel or knife, cut into 1½-inch squares and place on the baking sheets.

6   Bake for 6 to 7 minutes until very lightly browned, then transfer to wire racks to cool.

7   Meanwhile, make the filling. Put the cornstarch in a small pan. Blend in the milk until smooth. Add the butter and confectioners' sugar and bring to a boil, stirring constantly until thick.

8   Beat in the egg yolk and cream, cover and leave until cold.

9   Sandwich the cookies together and store in a cool place.

Strawberry Cheesecakes

1   Preheat the oven to 350°F. Lightly grease 2 or 3 baking sheets.

2   Put the butter and sugar in a bowl and beat until light and creamy. Beat in the egg yolk.

3   Mix together the flours, then add to the bowl. Mix in thoroughly to make a smooth dough. Knead gently.

4   On a lightly floured surface, roll out the dough to ⅛ inch thick. Cut out circles with a 2¼-inch fluted cutter. Place on baking sheets and remove centers from half of the circles with a petits fours cutter. Knead and re-roll trimmings to cut out more circles and tops until all the dough is used up.

5   Bake for 7 to 8 minutes until lightly browned. Transfer to wire racks to cool.

6   To make the filling, mix together cheese and cream. Spread a layer of cheese mixture and a layer of jam on the biscuit circles and top with rings. Keep in a cool place.

COOK'S TIP
The cheese filling softens these cookies quite quickly. To keep them crisp, do not fill more than 3 hours before serving.

INGREDIENTS

Makes 20

½ cup butter

6 tbsp sugar

1 egg yolk, beaten

¾ cup self-rising flour

½ cup whole wheat flour

⅔ cup soft cheese

1½ tbsp light cream

5 oz strawberry jam

Honey Brandy Snaps

INGREDIENTS

Makes 28

6 tbsp butter

6 tbsp light brown sugar

¼ cup light corn syrup

2 tbsp honey

¾ cup all-purpose flour

1 tsp ground ginger

finely grated zest of ½
lemon

1 tbsp brandy

1¼ cups whipping cream

2 tbsp honey

finely grated zest of ½
lemon

2 tsp lemon juice

1   Preheat the oven to 375°F. Line several baking sheets with nonstick baking parchment.

2   Put the butter, sugar, corn syrup and honey into a pan and stir over low heat until melted. Leave to cool slightly.

3   Sift together the flour and ginger. Stir into the melted ingredients with the lemon zest and brandy.

4   Drop 28 teaspoonfuls of the batter onto the baking sheets, spacing them well apart, then flatten slightly. Bake for 7 to 8 minutes until lightly browned.

5   Leave the brandy snaps to cool for a few seconds before rolling them around wooden spoon handles or pencils. Place on wire racks to cool completely.

6   To make the filling, whip the cream until standing in soft peaks. Add the honey, lemon zest and juice and whip until thick.

7   Spoon the cream into a decorating bag fitted with a small star tip. Pipe into the brandy snaps.

COOK'S TIP
Cook these in batches of 4 or 5 at a time as they must be shaped while hot. If they harden before shaping, reheat for a few seconds. To keep them crisp, do not fill more than an hour before serving.

Tia Maria Tuiles

1   Preheat the oven to 350°F. Line several baking sheets with nonstick baking parchment.

2   Put the egg whites in a clean, grease-free bowl. Beat until just stiff, then gradually beat in the sugar.

3   Fold in the butter and flour. Dissolve the coffee granules in Tia Maria, then stir gently into the batter.

4   Drop teaspoonfuls of the batter onto the baking sheets, spacing them well apart. Spread into 2-inch circles. Bake for 7 to 8 minutes until lightly browned around the edges.

5   Remove cookies from the baking sheets immediately and curve gently over rolling pins to shape.

6   Leave to cool slightly before transferring to wire racks to cool. Dredge with confectioners' sugar.

COOK'S TIP

Tuiles are crisp, thin cookies named after curved tiles whose shape they resemble. Cook in batches of only 6 or 7 at a time as they must be shaped while hot. If the cookies harden before shaping, return them to the oven for a few seconds to soften slightly.

INGREDIENTS

Makes 40

3 egg whites

7 tbsp sugar

6 tbsp butter, melted

5 tbsp all-purpose flour, sifted

¾ tsp instant coffee granules

4 tsp Tia Maria

confectioners' sugar to dredge

Muesli Cookies

INGREDIENTS

Makes 24

½ cup butter

6 tbsp light brown sugar

1 egg, beaten

¾ cup all-purpose flour

1 cup muesli breakfast cereal

½ cup blanched almonds, finely ground

1   Preheat the oven to 375°F. Lightly grease 2 or 3 baking sheets.

2   Put the butter and sugar in a bowl and beat until light and creamy. Beat in the egg.

3   Sift in the flour, then add the muesli and ground almonds and mix thoroughly.

4   Drop 24 heaped teaspoonfuls of mixture onto the baking sheets, spacing them well apart. Flatten slightly.

5   Bake for about 10 minutes or until lightly browned. Transfer to a wire rack to cool.

COOK'S TIP
Use a Swiss-style muesli for best results.

Linz Lattice

1   Lightly grease a shallow 11 x 7-inch pan.

2   Put the butter and sugar in a bowl and beat until light and creamy. Gradually beat in the egg and almond extract.

3   Sift together the flours and apple pie spice. Work into the creamed mixture with the ground almonds to make a soft dough. Knead lightly.

4   Cut off two-thirds of the dough and, on a lightly floured surface, roll out this portion of the dough to fit into the prepared pan. Press in well and spread the jam over the dough.

5   Roll out the remaining piece of dough to ⅙ inch thick. Cut into ½-inch strips. Arrange the strips in a lattice pattern over the jam. Chill for 30 minutes. Meanwhile, preheat the oven to 350°F.

6   Brush the lattice with milk and bake for 20 minutes or until lightly browned.

7   Leave to cool slightly in the tin. Cut into 3 pieces lengthwise and 5 widthwise to make 15 squares. Leave to cool completely, then dredge with confectioners' sugar.

INGREDIENTS

Makes 15

½ cup butter

¾ cup confectioners' sugar, sifted

1 egg, beaten

few drops of almond extract

1 cup all-purpose flour

½ cup self-rising flour

¾ tsp apple pie spice

¾ cup blanched almonds, finely ground

2½ tbsp raspberry jam

milk to glaze

confectioners' sugar to dredge

Hazelnut Florentines

INGREDIENTS

Makes 16

¼ cup butter

¼ cup sugar

1½ tbsp light corn syrup
½ tbsp honey

3 tbsp all-purpose flour

¾ cup chopped roasted
hazelnuts

⅓ cup candied cherries,
chopped

⅓ cup golden raisins

2 tbsp cut mixed candied
peel
finely grated zest of ½
lemon

2 oz each semisweet, milk,
and white chocolates

1   Preheat the oven to 350°F. Line several baking sheets with nonstick baking parchment.

2   Put the butter, sugar, corn syrup and honey into a pan and stir over low heat until melted. Cool slightly. Stir the flour into the melted mixture with the nuts, fruit and lemon zest.

3   Drop 16 heaped teaspoonfuls onto baking sheets, spacing well apart. Shape into neat circles. Bake for 10 to 11 minutes until lightly browned, then leave to stand for a few minutes before transferring to a wire rack to cool.

4   To finish the Florentines, melt each type of chocolate in individual small bowls placed over a pan of hot water. Spread the chocolate over the smooth side of each Florentine. Mark into wavy lines with a fork. Leave in a cool place to set.

COOK'S TIP
Use a good-quality chocolate for the best finish and melt it carefully. The bowl should fit the top of the pan exactly and should not touch the water beneath it. Use hot, not boiling water.

Sugar Pretzels

1   Lightly grease several baking sheets.

2   Put the butter and sugar in a bowl and beat until light and creamy. Beat in the egg, corn syrup, honey and vanilla extract.

3   Sift flour into bowl and mix in to make a smooth dough. Knead lightly. Divide the dough into 40 pieces on a floured surface. Roll each piece into a thin strand about 10 inches long.

4   To shape pretzels, tie each strand in a loose knot and press the ends near to the top of each circle. Place on the baking sheets and chill for 30 minutes.

5   Meanwhile, preheat the oven to 375°F. Bake the pretzels for 9 to 10 minutes until very lightly browned, then transfer to wire racks to cool.

6   When cool, brush the pretzels with egg white and sprinkle with brown sugar.

7   Place under a hot broiler for about 1 minute until the sugar is just starting to bubble and brown. Return to wire racks to cool.

INGREDIENTS

Makes 40

½ cup butter

1 cup confectioners' sugar, sifted

1 egg, beaten

2 tsp light corn syrup

1 tsp honey　.

few drops vanilla extract

2¼ cups all-purpose flour

To finish

1 egg white, beaten

⅓ cup light brown sugar

Caribbean Whirls

INGREDIENTS

Makes 30

½ cup butter

6 tbsp sugar

1 egg yolk

1¾ cups all-purpose flour

⅔ cup shredded coconut

For the buttercream

1 cup confectioners'
sugar, sifted

¼ cup butter

2 tbsp whipping cream

2 to 3 tsp dark rum

extra raisins and finely
grated orange and lime
zests to decorate

1   Preheat the oven to 350°F. Lightly grease 2 or 3 baking sheets.

2   Put the butter and sugar in a bowl and beat until light and creamy. Beat in the egg yolk.

3   Sift the flour into the bowl and add the coconut. Mix to make a soft dough and knead gently. Divide into 30 pieces and roll each piece into a ball. Place on the baking sheets and flatten slightly.

4   Bake for 16 to 18 minutes until lightly browned, then transfer to wire racks to cool.

5   Meanwhile, make the buttercream. Put the confectioners' sugar, butter and cream in a bowl and beat until light and creamy. Add rum to taste. Spoon into a decorating bag fitted with a small star tip.

6   Pipe whirls of buttercream onto the cookies and decorate with raisins and orange and lime zest. Store in a cool place.

Chocolate Chip Crescents

1   Lightly grease 2 baking sheets.

2   Put the butter and sugar in a bowl and beat until light and creamy. Sift in the flours and work in by hand to make a soft dough. Gently knead in the chocolate pieces.

3   On a lightly floured surface, roll out the dough to ⅓ inch thick. Cut out crescents with a 2½-inch cutter and place on the baking sheets. Knead and re-roll trimmings to cut out more crescents until the dough is used up. Chill for 30 minutes.

4   Meanwhile, preheat oven to 325°F. Bake the cookies for 20 to 25 minutes until very lightly browned, then transfer to a wire rack to cool.

5   Melt the chocolate in a small bowl placed over a pan of hot water. Coat half of each crescent with melted chocolate and place on a sheet of foil or nonstick baking parchment. Leave to set.

INGREDIENTS

Makes 24

½ cup butter

3 tbsp sugar

1 cup + 1 tbsp all-purpose flour

¼ cup rice flour

½ cup semisweet chocolate pieces

4 oz semisweet chocolate to finish

Apple Crumbles

INGREDIENTS

Makes 16

2 cups all-purpose flour

½ cup butter, chilled and diced

2 tbsp light brown sugar

2 egg yolks, beaten

For the topping

1 cup all-purpose flour

1 tsp ground cinnamon

¼ cup butter, chilled and diced

1 large dessert apple

2 tsp lemon juice

¼ cup light brown sugar

1   Preheat the oven to 325°F. Lightly grease 2 x 7-inch cake pans.

2   To make the base, sift the flour into a bowl. Cut in the butter until the mixture resembles fine bread crumbs. Stir in the sugar. Add the egg yolks and mix to make a firm dough. Knead gently.

3   Divide the dough into 2 pieces. On a lightly floured surface, roll out each piece to fit the sandwich pans. Press in well. Bake for 20 minutes.

4   Meanwhile, prepare the topping. Sift the flour and cinnamon into a bowl. Cut in the butter until the mixture resembles fine bread crumbs.

5   Finely grate the apple and toss in lemon juice. Stir into the cut-in mixture with the sugar.

6   Spoon the topping over the bases and return to the oven for about 35 minutes until browned. Mark each circle into 8 pieces and leave to cool in the pans.

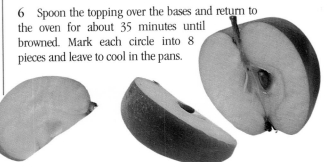

Viennese Pinks

1   Preheat the oven to 350°F. Lightly grease several baking sheets.

2   Put the butter and sugar in a bowl and beat until light and creamy. Add the strawberry flavoring. Sift in the flour and cornstarch and work in well.

3   Spoon the dough into a decorating bag fitted with a medium star tip. Pipe 3-inch strips onto the baking sheets.

4   Bake for about 20 minutes until very lightly browned. Leave for a few minutes before transferring to a wire rack to cool.

5   Melt the chocolate in a small bowl placed over a pan of hot water. Dip the ends of each cookie in chocolate and place on a sheet of foil or nonstick baking parchment. Leave to set.

COOK'S TIPS
If the dough is too stiff to pipe, soften with a few drops of milk.

INGREDIENTS

Makes 24

1 cup butter

½ cup confectioners' sugar, sifted

1¾ cups all-purpose flour

¾ cup cornstarch

a little strawberry flavoring

4 oz white chocolate to decorate

Choc and Oat Surprises

INGREDIENTS

Makes 20

½ cup butter

6 tbsp sugar

¾ cup self-rising flour

1 tbsp unsweetened cocoa
powder

⅔ cup quick-cooking
oatmeal + 2 tbsp for
coating

3 oz almond paste

½ cup semisweet
chocolate drops or pieces

1   Preheat the oven to 375°F. Lightly grease 2 baking sheets.

2   Put the butter and sugar in a bowl and beat until light and creamy. In another bowl, sift together the flour and cocoa powder. Add to the creamed mixture with the oatmeal and work in to make a fairly firm dough.

3   Divide both the dough and the almond paste into 20 pieces. Roll the almond paste pieces into balls and wrap a piece of dough around each one, pressing it gently over the almond paste.

4   Roll each ball in oatmeal to coat and place on the baking sheets. Top with chocolate drops or pieces.

5   Bake for about 10 minutes, or until just firm to touch. Transfer to a wire rack to cool.

Triple Chocolate Triangles

1   Put the butter and sugar in a bowl and beat until light and creamy. Sift in the flour, cornstarch and cocoa powder and work in well to make a smooth dough. Knead lightly.

2   On a lightly floured surface, roll out the dough to fit an 11 x 7-inch baking pan. Press in lightly and chill for 30 minutes.

3   Meanwhile, preheat the oven to 325°F. Bake for about 25 minutes or until just firm to touch.

4   Leave to cool for a few minutes, then mark into squares, cutting into 4 lengthwise and 6 widthwise. Cut each square into 2 triangles and leave to cool in the pan.

5   To finish, melt the semisweet chocolate in a small bowl over a pan of hot water. Dip the cookie triangles in the chocolate to coat evenly. Place on a sheet of foil or nonstick baking parchment and leave in a cool place to set.

6   Melt the white chocolate in the same way and pipe or drizzle over the cookie triangles. Leave in a cool place to set.

INGREDIENTS

Makes 48

1 cup butter

1 cup confectioners' sugar, sifted

1¾ cups all-purpose flour

½ cup cornstarch

2 tbsp unsweetened cocoa powder

To finish

1 lb semisweet chocolate, chopped

3 oz white chocolate

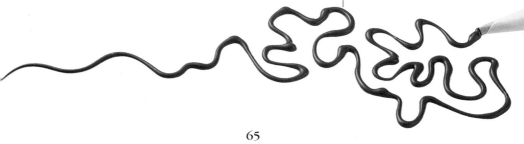

Almond Hearts

Makes 80

1 cup + 2 tbsp blanched almonds, finely ground

6 tbsp sugar

½ cup confectioners' sugar, sifted

1 egg, beaten

2 tsp brandy

extra beaten egg to glaze

¼ cup slivered almonds

1   Preheat the oven to 350°F. Line 2 or 3 baking sheets with nonstick baking parchment.

2   Put the ground almonds, sugar and confectioners' sugar into a bowl. Mix together. Stir in the egg and brandy to make a firm dough. Knead very lightly.

3   On a lightly floured surface, roll out the dough to ¼ inch thick. Brush with egg to glaze and sprinkle with slivered almonds.

4   Cut out shapes with a small heart-shaped cutter and place on the baking sheets. Push trimmings together to keep slivered almonds on top and cut out more hearts until all the dough is used up.

5   Bake for 10 to 12 minutes until lightly browned, then transfer to wire racks to cool.

Mother's Day Flowers

1   Preheat the oven to 350°F. Lightly grease 2 baking sheets.

2   Put the butter and sugar in a bowl and beat until light and creamy. Beat in the egg yolks.

3   Sift in flour, then add the cream and work in well.

4   Spoon the dough into a decorating bag fitted with a medium star tip. Pipe 12 flower shapes onto the baking sheets.

5   Bake for 12 to 14 minutes until lightly browned. Leave to stand for a few minutes, then transfer to a wire rack to cool.

6   Meanwhile, make the topping. In a small bowl, blend the confectioners' sugar with the rose or orange-flower water until smooth and fairly thick. Use to top cookies, creating a neat, even surface.

7   Decorate with candied flower pieces and orange zest and leave to dry.

INGREDIENTS

Makes 12

¼ cup butter

3 tbsp sugar

2 egg yolks, beaten

1 cup self-rising flour

4 tsp light cream

To decorate

½ cup confectioners' sugar, sifted

1½ to 2 tsp rose water or orange-flower water

candied flower pieces and finely grated orange zest

Easter Cookies

INGREDIENTS

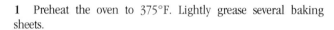

Makes 10

½ cup butter

6 tbsp sugar

1 egg, beaten

2 cups all-purpose flour

½ tsp apple pie spice

½ tsp ground cinnamon

⅓ cup currants

⅓ cup cut mixed candied peel

sugar to dredge

1 Preheat the oven to 375°F. Lightly grease several baking sheets.

2 Put the butter and sugar in a bowl and beat until light and creamy. Gradually beat in the egg.

3 Sift in flour, cinnamon and apple pie spice. Add the currants and peel, then mix to make a firm dough and knead lightly.

4 On a lightly floured surface, roll out the dough to ¼ inch thick. Cut out circles with a 4-inch fluted cutter and place on the baking sheets. Knead and re-roll trimmings to cut out more circles until all the dough is used up.

5 Bake for 15 minutes until or lightly browned. Dredge with sugar and transfer to a wire rack to cool.

Mocha Meringue Eggs

1   Preheat the oven to 275°F. Line 2 baking sheets with nonstick baking parchment.

2   Put the egg white in a clean, grease-free bowl. Beat until stiff but not dry. Gradually beat in half of the sugar. Fold in the remainder with the chocolate and cornstarch.

3   Drop rounded tablespoonfuls of the mixture onto the baking sheets and smooth into half-egg shapes. Bake for 50 to 55 minutes until firm to the touch. Leave to cool on the baking sheets.

4   Meanwhile, make the filling. Put the coffee and water in a small bowl and stir to dissolve. Melt the chocolate in a bowl placed over a pan of hot water. Whip half the cream until standing in soft peaks. Beat the remainder into the melted chocolate with the coffee until thick. Fold in the remaining whipped cream.

5   Spoon the chocolate cream into a decorating bag fitted with a small star tip. Pipe some cream onto the flat sides of the meringue eggs to sandwich together. Decorate with the remainder.

6   Tie ribbons around the eggs to finish. Keep chilled.

INGREDIENTS

Makes 8

2 egg whites

¾ cup + 2 tbsp sugar

4 oz semisweet chocolate, grated

½ cup cornstarch, sifted

For the filling

4 tsp instant coffee granules

2 tsp warm water

4 oz semisweet chocolate

⅔ cup whipping cream

Halloween Faces

INGREDIENTS

Makes 12

½ cup butter

4 tbsp sugar

1 ¼ cups all-purpose flour

2 tsp unsweetened cocoa powder, sifted

1   Preheat the oven to 375°F. Lightly grease 2 or 3 baking sheets.

2   Put the butter and sugar in a bowl and beat until light and creamy. Sift in the flour and work in to make a soft dough. Knead lightly.

3   Divide the dough in half on a floured surface. Knead the cocoa powder into one half.

4   Roll out each half of the dough to ⅓ inch thick. Using a sharp knife, cut out 3-inch faces and place on baking sheets. Cut out eye triangles and mouths from the trimmings and press gently onto the faces. Knead and re-roll the trimmings to cut out more faces until all the dough is used up.

5   Bake for about 8 minutes or until just firm to the touch. Leave to stand for a few minutes before transferring to a wire rack to cool.

Christmas Trees

1   Lightly grease 2 or 3 baking sheets.

2   Put the butter and sugar in a bowl and beat until light and creamy. Mix together the flours in another bowl, then add to the mixture and work in to make a soft dough. Knead gently.

3   On a floured surface, roll out the dough to ⅙ inch thick. Cut out trees about 3½ inches tall and place on the baking sheets. Knead and re-roll the trimmings to cut out more trees until all the dough is used up. Chill for 30 minutes.

4   Meanwhile, preheat the oven to 350°F. Bake the cookies for about 12 minutes until very lightly browned.

5   Transfer to a wire rack to cool, then decorate with confectioners' sugar.

COOK'S TIP
Use templates made from thin cardboard to mask centers or edges of Christmas trees, then dredge with confectioners' sugar to decorate.

INGREDIENTS

Makes 24

½ cup butter

3 tbsp light brown sugar

½ cup whole wheat flour

½ cup all-purpose flour, sifted

¼ cup rice flour, sifted

confectioners' sugar to decorate

Scandinavian Spiced Cookies

INGREDIENTS

Makes 18

¼ cup butter

2 tbsp light corn syrup
½ tbsp honey

3 tbsp light brown sugar

1 cup + 2 tbsp all-
purpose flour

¾ tsp apple pie spice

½ tsp baking soda

½ egg yolk

finely grated zest of ½
lemon

about ½ an egg white

¾ to 1 cup confectioners'
sugar, sifted

food colorings, candies

1   Preheat the oven to 350°F. Lightly grease 2 baking sheets.

2   Put the butter, corn syrup, honey and sugar into a pan and stir over low heat until melted. Leave to cool slightly.

3   Sift together the flour, apple pie spice and baking soda. Mix into the melted ingredients with the egg yolk and lemon zest.

4   Turn out the dough onto a floured surface and knead lightly. Roll out to ¼ inch thick and cut out shapes about 2½ inches in size using tree cutters. Place on the baking sheets. Using a skewer, make a small hole near the top of each cookie. Knead and re-roll trimmings to cut out more shapes.

5   Bake for 12 to 14 minutes until lightly browned. Push a skewer through each hole again to ensure they are large enough to thread ribbons through. Transfer to a wire rack to cool.

6   Meanwhile, make the frosting. Beat the egg white until frothy. Gradually beat in the sugar until smooth and thick.

7   Color if wished and spread or pipe onto the cookies. Decorate with candies and leave to dry.

8   Thread the cookies with ribbons to hang on the Christmas tree or pack to give as gifts.

Chocolate Crackers

1 Preheat the oven to 350°F. Line several baking sheets with nonstick baking parchment.

2 Put the egg whites in a clean, grease-free bowl. Beat until just stiff, then gradually beat in the sugar. Fold in the butter and flour.

3 Drop small tablespoonfuls of meringue onto the baking sheets, spacing them well apart. Spread into 4-inch circles. Bake for 7 to 8 minutes until lightly browned around the edges.

4 Immediately remove the cookies from the baking sheets and roll around pencils to shape. Place on a wire rack to cool.

5 Meanwhile, make the filling. Melt the chocolate and butter with brandy to taste in a small bowl over a pan of hot water. Remove from the heat and stir in confectioners' sugar and cream. Leave to cool, then chill until thick enough to pipe.

6 Spoon the filling into a decorating bag fitted with a ¼-inch plain round tip. Pipe into the centers of the rolled cookies. Wrap the cookies in colored foil to make crackers.

COOK'S TIP
Cook these in batches of 4 or 5 as they have to be handled while still hot.

INGREDIENTS

Makes 20

3 egg whites

7 tbsp sugar

6 tbsp butter, melted

½ cup all-purpose flour, sifted

For the filling

2 oz semisweet chocolate

1 tbsp butter

1 to 2 tsp brandy

¼ cup confectioners' sugar, sifted

2 tbsp light cream

Amaretti

INGREDIENTS

Makes 30

1 egg white

1½ tsp Amaretto liqueur

1¾ cups confectioners' sugar

1 cup sweet almonds, blanched and finely ground

1½ tbsp bitter almonds, blanched and finely ground

finely grated zest of ½ lemon

confectioners' sugar to dredge

colored tissue paper if wrapping

1 Preheat the oven to 350°F. Line 2 or 3 baking sheets with nonstick baking parchment.

2 Beat together the egg white and Amaretto liqueur.

3 Sift the confectioners' sugar into another bowl. Add all the ground almonds and the lemon zest. Make a well in the center. Pour in the egg white and mix to make a paste.

4 Divide the paste into 30 pieces and roll each piece into a ball. Place on the baking sheets. Bake for 12 to 15 minutes until lightly browned.

5 Dredge with confectioners' sugar and transfer to wire racks to cool. Wrap in tissue paper to pack if giving as gifts.

COOK'S TIP
If you cannot get bitter almonds use all sweet ones.

Snowballs

1   Put the chocolate, butter and brandy in a heatproof bowl. Place over a pan of hot water, stirring occasionally, until melted.

2   Stir the cracker crumbs, coconut, apricots and cherries into the melted mixture. Leave until slightly firm.

3   Roll the mixture into 18 balls about the size of walnuts, then roll in extra coconut to coat.

4   Refrigerate for about 2 hours until firmly set.

INGREDIENTS

Makes 18

8 oz white chocolate, chopped

¼ cup butter

4 tsp brandy

⅔ cup Graham cracker crumbs

3 tbsp shredded coconut

¼ cup ready-to-eat dried apricots, finely chopped

¼ cup candied cherries, finely chopped

an extra 3 tbsp shredded coconut for rolling

Toffee Fingers

INGREDIENTS

Makes 12

5 tbsp light corn syrup

1 tbsp honey

⅓ cup light brown sugar

3 tbsp butter

1 cup crisp rice breakfast
cereal

For the filling

6 oz cream toffee candies

¼ cup butter

¼ cup light cream

For the topping

3 oz milk chocolate

2 tbsp butter

1   Lightly grease a shallow, 7-inch baking pan. Line the bottom with nonstick baking parchment.

2   To make the base, put the corn syrup, honey, brown sugar and butter into a pan. Stir over low heat until melted. Bring to a boil. Stir in the cereal, then press into the prepared pan.

3   To make the filling, put the toffee candies, butter and cream into a pan. Stir over low heat until melted. Bring to a boil. Pour the filling over the base. Refrigerate for about 1 hour until set.

4   To make the topping, put the chocolate and butter into a heatproof bowl. Place over a pan of hot water, stirring occasionally, until melted.

5   Spread the topping over the toffee-flavored filling and refrigerate for about 1 hour until set.

6   Carefully invert the slab from the pan and peel off the paper. Cut the square in half and cut each half into 6 fingers. Keep refrigerated until serving.

Tropical Treats

1   Lightly grease a shallow, square 8-inch baking pan. Line the bottom with nonstick baking parchment.

2   Put the butter, corn syrup, honey, cocoa powder and coffee into a pan and stir over low heat until melted.

3   Stir in the cereal, banana chips, coconut and raisins. Turn into the prepared pan and press down well. Refrigerate for 2 to 3 hours until firmly set.

4   Carefully invert the slab from the pan and peel off the paper. Cut into 3 each way to make squares. Cut each square into 2 triangles to serve.

COOK'S TIP
Keep no-bake cookies in a container in the refrigerator for up to 10 days.

INGREDIENTS

Makes 18

½ cup butter

3 tbsp light corn syrup

1 tbsp honey

1 ½ tbsp unsweetened cocoa powder

2 tsp instant coffee granules

4 cups crunchy oat cereal, crushed

⅓ cup ready-to-eat banana chips, chopped

⅔ cup shredded coconut

⅓ cup raisins, chopped

Date and Walnut Slices

Makes 20

½ cup butter

2 tbsp brown sugar

2 tbsp light corn syrup

1 tbsp honey

finely grated zest of ½
lemon

3 cups whole wheat cereal
flakes, lightly crushed

¾ cup pitted dates, finely
chopped

¾ cup walnuts, finely
chopped

1   Lightly grease a shallow, square 8-inch baking pan. Line the bottom with nonstick baking parchment.

2   Put the butter, sugar, corn syrup, honey and lemon zest into a pan. Stir over low heat until melted.

3   Stir in the cereal, dates and walnuts. Pour into the prepared pan and press down well. Refrigerate for 2 to 3 hours until set.

4   Carefully invert the slab from the pan and peel off the paper. Cut into 4 slices, then cut each slice into 5 pieces. Keep refrigerated until serving.

Orange Muesli Bars

1 Lightly grease a shallow, square 8-inch baking pan. Line the bottom with nonstick baking parchment.

2 Break the chocolate into pieces. Put it into a saucepan with the butter, honey, and orange zest and juice. Stir over low heat until melted.

3 Stir in the muesli. Turn into the prepared pan and press down well. Refrigerate for 2 to 3 hours until firmly set.

4 Carefully invert the slab from the pan and peel off the paper. Cut the square in half, then cut each half into 8 bars to serve.

COOK'S TIP
In this recipe, chocolate can safely be melted directly over heat in the pan. The addition of a large quantity of other ingredients prevents it from scorching.

INGREDIENTS

Makes 16

8 oz semisweet chocolate

½ cup butter

4 tbsp honey

finely grated zest of 2 oranges

4 tbsp orange juice

4 cups Swiss-style muesli breakfast cereal

Index

EAT, DRINK AND BE MERRY,
FOR TOMORROW WE LIVE

EAT, DRINK AND BE MERRY, FOR TOMORROW WE LIVE

Studies in Christianity and Development

MICHAEL TAYLOR

T&T CLARK INTERNATIONAL
A Continuum imprint
LONDON • NEW YORK

Published by T&T Clark International

A Continuum imprint

The Tower Building, 11 York Road, London SE1 7NX
15 East 26th Street, Suite 1703, New York, NY 10010

www.tandtclark.com

British Library Cataloguing-in-Publication Data
A catalogue record for this book is available from the British Library

ISBN 0567030326 (paperback)

Typeset by Data Standards Ltd, Frome, Somerset BA11 1RE
Printed on acid-free paper in Great Britain by
Antony Rowe Ltd, Chippenham, Wilts.

Dedicated in gratitude
to the memory of
Ronald H. Preston
1913–2001
teacher, mentor and friend

Contents

Acknowledgments

My thanks are due to those who invited me to give these papers and discussed them with me. Very special thanks to Wendy Tyndale and Maggie Clay who, in their different ways, contributed so much to the work which made many of these pages possible.

A shorter version of Chapter 4 was included in *Globalization and the Good*, edited by Peter Heslam (London: SPCK, 2004). Chapter 6 originally appeared in *The Future of Social Ethics. A Special Issue of Studies in Christian Ethics*, 17/ 2 (2004).

Michael Taylor
October 2004

Abbreviations

AMAN	Asian Muslim Action Network
CAFOD	Catholic Agency for Overseas Development
CARE	Community AIDS Response
CIYA	Cambodian Islamic Youth Association
CWM	Council for World Mission
DFLD	Department for International Development [UK]
GNP	gross national product
GUP	Gono Unnayan Prochesta
HIPC	highly indebted poor countries
IFF	International Finance Facility
IFI	International Financial Institution
IMF	International Monetary Fund
IT	information technology
LEP	local ecumenical project
MDGs	Millennium Development Goals
NEPAD	New Economic Partnership for African Development
NGO	non-governmental organization
NU	Nahdlatul Ulama
ODI	Overseas Development Institute [of London]
PRSP	Poverty Reduction Strategy Paper
SAPs	structural adjustment policies
SSM	Sarvodaya Shramadan Movement
TINA	there is no alternative
TNC	transnational corporation
UK	United Kingdom
UN	United Nations
URC	United Reformed Church
USA	United States of America
VGKK	Vivekananda Girijana Kalyana Kendra
WCC	World Council of Churches
WDR	World Development Report
WTO	World Trade Organization

Introduction

Most of the essays in this book have been written during my time as Director of the World Faiths Development Dialogue set up in 1997 to foster interfaith dialogue and co-operation on poverty reduction and human development. Some of the recurring themes can be understood against that background. If, for example, I was aware of pluralism and relativism beforehand, I am even more aware of them now, having encountered the bewildering diversity that exists within other faith traditions as well as my own, and the many ways in which our views are influenced by, or relative to, the various circumstances out of which we speak.

It is this plurality which makes what I call 'radical participation', referred to more than once in what follows, or the effort, however difficult, to take many voices into account when decisions are made, so important. It not only matters for the sake of justice; it also matters if we are to be wise and not deny ourselves the wealth of insight, however partial, that lies within these wide-ranging views. Any traditions, including the Western tradition as discussed in Chapter 1, or the mainstream traditions of development as discussed in Chapter 7, which regard themselves as self-sufficient, not only fool themselves but impoverish themselves.

So far in these varied encounters I realize I have learned very little compared with all that there is to discover and appreciate. Without romanticizing about other faith traditions, which can be as open to criticism as my own, what I have learned has usually been refreshing and enriching, partly no doubt because it has come from people committed to the well-being of some of the poorest countries and communities – poor at least in material terms. Muslims and Buddhists, for example, have offered their insights on the economic order, on international debt and investments. More telling for me, and my somewhat secularized version of Christianity, has been the insistence of many faith traditions on the absolute importance of the spiritual dimension of development. Without denying the need for outward and structural change they are clear that it will add up to very little in the long run without a change of heart: a change that mainstream approaches to development have done little to bring about.

1

One shift of emphasis that I discern in myself and in these essays has to do with what is sometimes referred to as the need to move from 'opposition' to 'proposition'. In a sense the development movement of the last 50 years has always been positive in its aims but its campaigning voice often comes over as negative in tone, highly critical of a world order which leaves all too many marginalized and near-destitute. The Christian Realism which nurtured me, and which is another recurring theme of these essays, can also be heard to strike a negative note. It is never over-confident that human beings will do the right thing by their neighbours, especially when their own interests are at stake and their neighbours, near and far, are weaker than they are. It is important, therefore, to be realistic and at least to protect the neighbour by means that have to do, for example, with power structures and legislation. So we protest and protect against the worst; and very much need, in the face of sentimental and moral appeals which go largely unheeded, to be better behaved towards each other.

Realism and experience suggest, however, that there is another side to human nature, which is not only compassionate but also creative and capable of imagining and making a different kind of world even if never complete or perfect. I think I have learned to appreciate the importance and the possibility of being constructive rather more than I once did.

All of the chapters which follow began life as 'public' lectures given in the UK, and are reproduced more or less as delivered, retaining a sense of time and place and of the other boundaries which contain us all. I have not tried to remove all repetitions in the hope that they will at least indicate some of the themes which matter most to me, including the issues to which I have just referred.

'Eat, Drink and Be Merry, for Tomorrow We Live' (Chapter 1) was addressed to the Methodist Conference in Ipswich in June 2001, at the invitation of its president for that year. It picks up on a rather brave remark of her own about the death of Methodism and suggests that is not just Methodism but much of Western Christianity which may well be exhausted and incapable of renewing itself from within. Having pointed to a number of blind alleys, I suggest that a rule of thumb for the future might be to do nothing without crossing boundaries, including among others the boundaries with other faiths, not just for the sake of it but in order to seek together the common good.

'Why Development Matters to the North' (Chapter 2) was my contribution to the attempt by the Churches World Development Network in May 2001 to write a letter encouraging greater commitment by all and sundry to eradicating poverty and injustice. It was an interesting device for clearing our heads. I suggested that the letter should appeal to the self-interests of the North (in the spirit of my Christian Realism) and also to its moral sense, its compassion (moved, as we still can be, not by arguments and statistics but by human stories) and its need for inspiration and vision.

'Facing Up to Reality: The Future of the Poor' (Chapter 3) was a lecture to the Manchester Theological Society in February 2002, repeated at Regent's Park College, Oxford and at Leeds University. It tries to come to terms with the fact that there are highly divergent views about reality, including whether the global economy really works in favour of the poor or against them, why that is the case, and how therefore we should proceed. Decision-making, as has recently been attempted in the efforts of some of the poorest countries to draw up strategies for poverty reduction, must be participatory and inclusive of a wide range of opinion, however difficult that may be; and the central issue of power and how to balance it out, even in consultative processes, cannot be avoided. Too often the negative view of the economy is under-standably held by those who have little power in the situation or say in what happens to them.

'Poverty and Globalization' (Chapter 4) was one of a series of lectures given in Wesley's Chapel in the City of London in April 2002. They were in preparation for activities by Christians on May Day which, in contrast to some violent anti-globalization protests, were to be entirely peaceful though critical of the role played by city institutions in the global economy. The lectures gave the campaigners their marching orders as it were. While standing firm against injustice, I suggested they should resist demonizing the opposition, take full account of the darker side of human nature and be preachers and promoters of attractive alternatives. A shortened version of what I said was published in *Globalization and the Good*, edited by Peter Heslam (London: SPCK, 2004).

'Rejection or Reform?' (Chapter 5) was a lecture to the Nottingham Theological Society in October 2003 arising out of encounters with radical Christian groups in Europe as well as the 'South' who seemed not simply to criticize the global economic order but to reject it altogether. Some even identified it as a Christian 'heresy'. Seeing myself as a 'reformist' rather than a 'rejectionist' I wondered whether in practice there was all that much difference between the two and how, nevertheless, 'rejectionists' could challenge 'reformists' and ensure that our analysis and reflection on the global economy goes deep enough.

'Faith in the Global Economic System' (Chapter 6) was one of the Samuel Ferguson lectures in the University of Manchester in 2003 and my contribution to a colloquium in March of that year on 'The Future of Christian Social Ethics', honouring and evaluating the work of R. H. Preston, who died in 2002. Most of the papers, including this one, were subsequently published in a special issue of *Studies in Christian Ethics*, 2004. Preston was concerned, among many other things, to see that Christian faith made a significant but appropriate contribution to social policy, respecting the necessary contributions of other disciplines, including economics. One method of doing so, much discussed in Preston's writings, was by way of 'middle axioms'. In an increasingly plural world the need to find common ground becomes even more important and some of Preston's recipes for being wise need taking further, while others – including middle axioms – now seem less helpful.

'King Mohosoth and Princess Amara' (Chapter 7) was the annual E. R. Wickham lecture, given in Manchester Cathedral in May 2004. It is a limited exercise in 'radical participation' and describes an encounter in New Delhi in February 2004 between 11 faith communities coming from four different faith traditions: Buddhist, Christian, Hindu and Muslim. The insights of these communities, reflected in case studies of their work with the poor, show a degree of convergence with the mainstream Western approach to development but also produce some sharp challenges. Most obvious among them is the insistence that development must be far more holistic and not merely economic. Above all, it must take seriously the spiritual dimension of human life and the need for 'inner transformation' as well as structural change. The Buddhist King and Princess of the title cannot do without each other.

The last few years have confirmed me in the view that, just as Christian ecumenism is best explored in the context of 'life and work', so interfaith dialogue is generally most productive when it is focused on human issues like poverty reduction and development and how together we can move them forward. There is little doubt these days that faith, including religious faith, has its part to play. If religion, especially in the West, had to fight for attention in the past, since 9/11 its significance is everywhere acknowledged. For good or ill it is seen to have a role. Too often its role is perceived to be negative or regressive, hindering rather than helping creative change. History meanwhile bears witness that it has served the poor well in many ways and any fair assessment suggests it has a great deal of capital – social, intellectual, moral and spiritual – to contribute to a common search for the good. One thing is clear, however: faith cannot hope to change the world for the better without itself being changed. 'Inner transformation' is not just for individuals. It is also for traditions and institutions. Faith can be an agent of reform but not without, in the process, being open to reform itself.

The title of this book is borrowed from Chapter 1 and alludes to a familiar aspect of faith, and that is hope. It is something which the world undoubtedly needs, but it is difficult to get right. It is clearly opposed to cynical despair; but it is likely to be extremely fragile if it relies too heavily on the signs of the times. For some it is a deep-seated conviction, which I respect even if I cannot easily share, that in the end all will be well: tomorrow we shall live, not die. For me, hope is essentially what we, and the God I know best in Christ, put into situations rather than take out of them. We believe they have potential for good, and by acting accordingly we increase that potential: in this case, that faith communities like the Christian Church can be part of a transformative enterprise which enables more and more of us to eat and drink as we need and to be 'merry' in the best sense of that word.

1

Eat, Drink and Be Merry, for Tomorrow We Live (cf. Luke 12.19)[1]

The demise of Methodism and of Western Christianity

In her presidential address to the Methodist Conference in 2001, Christina le Moignan 'came out' on the possibility of Methodism ceasing to exist in the not-too-distant future as a separate denomination. Not now the 'death of God' but the 'death of Methodism', even if it was a good death she had in mind.

My only quarrel is that if we are serious about our future under God we need to go wider than le Moignan has chosen to go. Methodism is obviously different from the other churches in Britain, but it cannot be separated from them. These churches, taken separately and together, are also obviously different from the other churches of Europe and the Northern and Western parts of the world, but they cannot be separated from them either. For all our ecumenical debates we are fundamentally more alike than unlike. We are recognizable, Methodism included, as belonging to one family or what I shall dare to call the 'Western Christian tradition', and it will not do for any of us to contemplate the possible demise of the Methodists, or the United Reformed Church (who openly declared a policy of euthanasia a generation ago), or the Baptists (who think they discern a sign of eternal life in slightly improving membership figures), or the demise of anyone else in isolation. We have to contemplate the demise of Western Christianity, or at least the possibility that this long and interesting, if not always honourable, tradition is now exhausted.

---

[1] Addressed to the Methodist Conference in Ipswich (UK) in June 2001.

I shall not take up too much time justifying that claim. Even if it's not true it's a useful stimulus to long-term thinking; but let me make one or two remarks to show that it is not entirely without foundation.

First, it is not just Methodism but Western Christianity that faces decline in numbers and influence and is trying to manage it. Some sectarian movements can point to bursts of energy but they do not alter the overall picture. Efforts to reorder ministry or to make ends meet or to reorganize the churches (my own Baptist denomination recently adopted the WCC-speak about 'clusters') are entirely understandable and to be supported. But they are unlikely to bring a new dawn. At one level they seem like the sensible thing to do; at another level they are like rearranging the deckchairs on the *Titanic*.

Second, the ecumenical movement within Western Christianity has dominated most of my life. I have believed in it passionately, not so much because it would improve the reputation of the Church if we united, or lead to the astonished conversion of the world, but because I thought it was the way to refresh and renew our faith and mission. Here and there, especially in some Local Ecumenical Partnership (LEPs), people will still say 'Amen' to that; one less discreet Methodist leader described ecumenical conversations as a bit of a 'yawn'. Overall I sense a distinct loss of momentum. Ecumenism struggles to come to terms with pluralism. I for one am no longer convinced that the ecumenical movement as we understood it, trying to overcome our differences mainly on Faith and Order issues and build the one great Church, is any longer the way forward, which is never to suggest that good relationships between churches don't matter.

Third, and of much greater significance for me, is the apparent impotence of Western Christianity. We could talk about this in rather chauvinistic terms and contrast the ways in which, say, the Free Churches of earlier generations were a force to be reckoned with when it came to the big public issues of the day with the sorry, antiseptic letter sent by the Archbishops of Canterbury and York to the people of the Church of England before the UK General Election of 2001. They seemed unable to speak out prophetically on any big issue at all. We could also talk about this impotence in terms of Christian social ethics and our increasing inability to add value to debates about social and political policies. We can certainly talk about it on the international stage. Western Christianity has exported itself vigorously to almost every corner

of the globe: through movements of empire, through colonization, through missionaries, through development workers,
through capitalist traders and financiers. It set out ostensibly to
redeem and civilize humankind and to establish justice and God's
kingdom throughout the earth. It has had an enormous impact
on history. Individuals caught up in it have done great good. But
at the end of the day it is difficult to see how the overall quality of
our life together is a great deal better than it was. Things do get
better; but things also get worse. Peace comes closer; but wars
break out. Genocide follows on the heels of holocaust. Fewer
children die in infancy; but more die from AIDS. The poor are
still with us. The gap between rich and poor grows wider. The
earth has not been filled with the 'glory of God' but 'environmental disaster' at the end of centuries of Christian missionary
endeavour; and the Gospel has not been notably successful in
turning round the sinners whose obstinacy is said to get in its way.
It is this scenario that has undermined my own theological
stability in recent years perhaps more that anything else.

A fourth and even more grandiose point could be added. Many
of the movements that spring from the European Enlightenment
are not to be lightly set aside in the way that some Christians these
days are all too fond of doing. The liberating power of reason over
the tyrannies of religion is not to be lightly set aside. The power of
science to solve problems is not to be lightly set aside. But the
Enlightenment had a grand design. It can be seen as the dawn of a
grand project to master the complexities of our world in an
overarching system inspired by reason. The most recent name we
have given it is 'globalization'. It is extremely difficult to extricate
Western Christianity from that project. All the poor communities I
know in the Third World, for example, cannot separate in their
minds Christianity from capitalism. The problem with an overarching, all-embracing system (as we have seen with ecumenism)
is that it can exclude as many as it includes. It cannot contain
everything so it rejects a great deal. It becomes imperial. It
represents the interest of the powerful and marginalizes the weak.
The signs are that the project is faltering as the world reasserts its
inevitable plurality, and that Western Christianity will falter with it.

So, if we wish to take a long-term view, we need to talk not just
about the possible demise of Methodism but the exhausted state
of Western Christianity, of which Methodists and Baptists and
some even stranger bedfellows are all a part.

Inevitable exhaustion

The first thing to be said about this is that it is not our fault, or indeed anybody's fault. Of course we *are* at fault in all sorts of ways. But the exhaustion of Western Christianity is not primarily a matter of personal failure, just as death is not usually a matter of personal failure. It is an unavoidable fact; and the fact is entirely in line with our Christian teaching on the one hand and our so-called 'postmodernist' understanding of the world on the other.

As Christians we are taught that we are mortal and not God. That is true of us as individuals and it is true of all the movements and institutions we fashion, including our Western forms of Christianity. They are bound at some point to fade. 'Our little systems have their day; they have their day and cease to be.'[2] They do not live for ever.

As to postmodernism, whatever else we make of it, it brings us sharply up against another aspect of our mortality. We are inevitably incomplete. Postmodernism reacts against the 'modern' world view because it tries to tell one single all-embracing story about our life in this world. There is no such story. There is no single explanation. There is no point of view into which all of us can fit, whether it's Western Christianity or secularism or scientific rationalism or Marxism or globalization or anything else. This is essentially a plural world. It is full of people and groups of people with different stories to tell about their lives and no possibility of telling the whole story about other people's lives. Every story or explanation or ideology or faith is partial and incomplete. It is incomplete because the way we see things depends on who we are, and where we come from, and what we have experienced. It is conditioned, or 'contextual', or 'relative', as they say, to our personalities, our cultures, our self-interests, our history and our experience. It doesn't mean we can't talk to one another at all, but it does mean that if we were different people, in a different place, at a different time, with a different history and different interests, we should talk in a different way. Change the conditions and you change the story.

Western Christianity is no exception. In a postmodern, pluralist world which understands that everything is coloured and conditioned by circumstance, it is seen as being inevitably incomplete.

---

[2] Alfred, Lord Tennyson, *In Memoriam A.H.H.* (1850) Prologue.

It is not self-sufficient and it is not surprising that, left to itself or keeping itself to itself, its resources will eventually run dry and it will suffer from exhaustion.

Some will quickly and understandably object that surely Christianity is different. It is the universal truth revealed to us by God through Jesus Christ. It is above this sea of relativism. It is not merely mortal; it has something about it of the divine. Its truths are final and universal; and if not Christianity then Jesus Christ himself, God incarnate, Word made flesh, is the absolute truth for all humankind.

I do not question in any way our unique and proper respect for our Lord Jesus Christ, but however unique and absolute we may believe him to be, how we see him and talk about him and interpret him, and the forms of Christianity we create and promote inspired by him, cannot escape from the conditioning factors we have been talking about. The many, many forms of Christianity in the Bible, throughout history and in the world today are evidence of that. So is the highly particular Methodist tradition and my own Baptist tradition. So is Western Christianity taken as a whole. In recent years we have not discovered contextual theology or faith; we have simply realized that all theologies and faiths, including all forms of Christianity, have always been contextual.

The seventeenth-century German hymn, 'Fairest Lord Jesus, Lord of all Creation', nicely illustrates the point. Verse 3 suggests an exception to the rule, and goes like this:

> Fairer the flowers, fairer still the sons of men,
> In all the freshness of youth arrayed:
> Yet is their beauty fading and fleeting;
> My Jesus, thine will never fade.[3]

The sons of men and all their works, including their forms of Christianity, are fading and fleeting; but not my Jesus. He will never fade. The irony of course is that the hymn, together with its picture of a never-fading Jesus, reflects a highly particular form of Christianity. We call it Early German Romanticism. It emphasized the emotional rather than the rational side of faith and was not necessarily the worse for that. It saw Jesus as close to nature, to meadows and woodlands and flowers. It was a beautiful and

---

[3] *The BBC Hymn Book* (Oxford: Oxford University Press, 1951), no. 138.

valuable and often moving point of view; but it was incomplete. This understanding of an unchanging Lord Jesus would fade like all the rest.

If Western Christianity does lie exhausted, it is not to be seen as our fault but as a fact. Our own faith teaches us that any form of faith is mortal, forever transcended by unknown realities greater than itself. Our postmodernist understanding of the world teaches us that it is relative and conditioned and therefore incomplete like everything else. It sees some things but not others; it understands in part but not altogether; it has a point of view but not a total view.

What we should worry about is not those who recognize that all forms of Christianity and faith are bound to fade and run out of steam, but those who believe their faith is above any such vulnerability. It is the absolutists and fundamentalists of this world who are the greater problem, and they are not only or always to be found in the official fundamentalist camps. All sorts of Christians think they have the last and only word; just like all sorts of Muslims and all sorts of economists in the World Bank and all sorts of fervent evangelists for the capitalist cause who have the audacity to describe the global economy as 'the End of History'. They all chant the same disastrous mantra: TINA, TINA: There Is No Alternative: no other way to our salvation. They all forget the mortality of their systems and how partial and incomplete they are. They are doubly dangerous because they often represent the powerful. Western Christianity is no exception. It has been characteristically the religion of the powerful since the early centuries. And the powerful are all too often the terrorists of truth. They impose the systems that suit them on everybody else. But the real pity of it all is not just their power but their inevitable self-impoverishment. They convince themselves that they are self-sufficient instead of recognizing that they are incomplete. They have no need of anything else. They rule out all the people and ways of thinking and believing about life that they marginalize. So they deny to themselves, and all the people they embrace and constrain, the riches available elsewhere. Left to themselves in their arrogance they have insufficient resources to help themselves. Their undoubted energy and insight can only flow out and away. They fail to see where their own health lies.

Dead ends

Which brings me to the second point I want to make about the exhaustion of Western Christianity, this form of Christian faith which has dominated Christian history for centuries as it moved out relentlessly across the world. There is no easy way forward towards new life; and while I shall try to be constructive, I shall not be suggesting one. Before coming to that, however, there are a number of dead ends to try to avoid. Here are five of them.

First, I have already suggested that Christian ecumenism as we have understood it for almost a century is a dead end on the road to renewal, which does not mean that good relations between Christian people don't matter. Second, I believe that sustaining the Church by recruitment evangelism or by church planting or by management techniques is a dead end on the road to renewal, which does not mean that caring for people and institutions and deploying resources effectively doesn't matter. Third, I believe that the attempt to go back to more 'authentic' forms of Christianity, whether charismatic or evangelical, radical or political, is a dead end on the road to renewal, which is not to say that a constant critical dialogue between our current forms of Christianity and their foundation texts, including the gospel pictures of Jesus, doesn't matter. Fourth, I believe that taking shelter in absolutisms or infallibilities, whether they are of a sectarian kind or recent claims that Christianity is 'public truth', as factual as any other and no more contestable, is a dead end on the road to renewal, which is not to say that women and men of conviction are not wanted on board. Fifth, I believe that merely restating Christian belief in the terms and language of the Western philosophies of the day, secular or postmodern or whatever, is a dead end on the road to renewal, which is not to say that the insights of the great thinkers of our day and our own grey matter are to be left on one side.

All five of these familiar attempts to find a way forward are dead ends for much the same reason. They are all attempts to revive an exhausted form of Christianity largely from within itself. They all reflect the same fundamental failure to recognize the nature of the problem. They assume there are sufficient resources within the tradition for the tradition to renew and revive itself, when the crisis which threatens its demise, and the demise of all our churches, is that its own internal resources may well be near exhaustion. We must be very careful indeed not to look for water in wells already running dry.

Looking for life

So now we have collected two dead parrots: a dead or dying Western Christianity, and a rather large road sign saying: 'Dead End'. The task, however, is to look for life. We need the open road that climbs the hill and reaches for the horizon and the sky.

I think that's what Methodists were looking for when they adopted the statement about 'Our Calling' at their Conference in 2000 in Huddersfield (UK): a calling to Worship, to Learning and Caring, to Service and to Evangelism. Similar statements have appeared in other churches. In my own it became known as the Five Marks of Mission. From what I have said already it should be clear why I don't quarrel with any of them but don't quite give 'three cheers' for them either.

In my earlier days as a Christian, when the ecumenical movement seemed to be the way forward, they coined a principle that tried to guide us along the road ahead. It was called the Lund Principle. It became very well known. It invited us 'to do everything together except where conscience required us to do it separately'. All too often we remained determined to do everything separately until an economic crisis forced us to do it together, but it nevertheless gave us a sense of direction which could help shape all the many and varied decisions we had to make.

Can we discover anything like a Lund Principle, or a set of principles, or some simple 'rules of thumb' which could help to shape 'our calling' today as we face up to the exhausted state of Western Christianity and search for new life?

I have two suggestions to make by way of being constructive. They are far from new. I hear them being distilled out of struggle and experience and practice in many places. They are part of a search. They are not meant to be simplistic or easy or romantic or final solutions to the huge and challenging questions we face as Western Christians. They might, however, help to set the agenda and shape our obedience.

Crossing boundaries

The language of the first, if not the substance, is borrowed from a stimulating book of essays published in 2000 by CWM (the Council for World Mission) called: *Plurality, Power and Mission.* The language is about 'crossing boundaries'. The rule of thumb or principle could be this: 'to do nothing without crossing boundaries', or, put more positively: 'to cross boundaries as a necessary part of everything we now do'. Let me say something about what the boundaries are, why we need to cross them, and some of the difficulties we shall face.

I can think of five examples of boundaries we need to cross. One is between Western Christianity and what we might call Southern Christianity: the Christianity of the so-called Third World, of Asia and Southern and Central America, of Africa and the Pacific, of the southern countries where most of the Christians of the twenty-first century are to be found. A century ago the majority were here in the north. Now up to 70 per cent of them are in the south. Of course a good deal of their Christianity is a barely recycled form of our own. Of course if we listen to them we shall often hear only echoes of our own exported voices. But there is also a very different voice to be heard. It has less to say about the forgiveness of personal sins, for example, and much more to say about the struggle for justice. It is the strange and often dissonant cry of the Minjung and the Dalit and the indigenous peoples of the Americas. It is the Christianity not of the powerful but of the poor. The context has changed. The point of view, however partial, is therefore different.

A second boundary is probably the most talked-about – and not surprisingly. It is between Western Christianity and other religious faiths. Many of them are now well represented in our multi-faith cities and towns: the faiths of our Muslim, Sikh, Hindu and Buddhist neighbours. It is when many of us are confronted by these boundaries that the plurality of the world seems so undeniable and any retreat into absolute and superior claims for Christianity so unhelpful and unrealistic. It seems like burying our heads in the sand.

Third is the boundary less talked about, between Western Christianity and non-religious faiths or ideologies. Again we can do little more than listen to echoes of our own voices since Western Christianity has been conditioned and relativized by so many of those ideologies itself, including the ideologies of progress and individualism and free-market capitalism. But there are people all over the world who have strong convictions about human life and society and wish to uphold humanitarian values and universal human rights and the rights of all living things, but do not care to express their faith in religious terms.

Fourth, there are what we might call the inter-disciplinary boundaries. Western Christianity has a lot to say about the nature of human beings and the so-called natural world, how they work and what their meanings and destinies may be. It's fairly quick to say all this when we stand, for example, on the frontiers of medical research and is not too keen on what it sees. But many other disciplines have much to say as well, from the scientific and medical to the technical, from the sociological to the philosophic. Some are familiar and have made their mark on Western Christianity. Others are not so familiar and come bearing strange information about our genetic past, our virtual-reality, computerized present, and about a cloneable future in cyber-space: the Gallileos of our time. It is strange territory for the Church.

A fifth example has to do with social boundaries. I am not sure whether they are characterized in economic terms of poverty and wealth, or class, or ethnic terms or in terms of the generations; but there are obvious boundaries between them and the Western Christian tradition, otherwise many on the other side of them would more obviously be at home in our institutions and we would not talk about them and about 'alienation' in one and the same breath.

The proposal is: 'to cross boundaries as a necessary part of everything we now do'. But why are these boundaries and so many others to be crossed? The answer is not the traditional answer of Christian mission. It has been busy crossing geographical and cultural boundaries ever since it set out from Jerusalem after Pentecost to go into all Judea and Samaria and away to the ends of the earth. The answer is not to correct and redeem what is on the other side of the boundary in order to replace it with the truth we already know, and extend our Christian territory into areas where it has not been established before.

The answer is that we have to cross these boundaries because our own understanding is partial and relative and incomplete and our resources are probably near exhaustion. The only way to get a better understanding and replenish our supplies is to open up to the equally partial and relative and incomplete understandings of those whose histories and experiences have been different from our own: to the poor, the communities of other faiths, the humanist, the secular scientist or social worker and the sub-cultures of our cities which can seem to be simply out of our world. They are no better than us and they are no more self-sufficient. They are no less partial and incomplete than we are, but their partiality is different. They see what we do not see, just as we see what they do not. Meeting them across the boundaries in the plurality of our postmodern world is not a matter of delivering our truth, but of allowing their incompleteness to begin to fill up our own and our incompleteness to begin to fill up theirs, so that together we not only critique and challenge each other but also enlarge and complement one another until the whole can become greater and more resourceful than our separate parts.

Let us be clear. Crossing boundaries has nothing to do with colonizing new territories, whether geographical, intellectual or social, with fresh outposts of Western Christianity. We are not extending boundaries, we are crossing them. It is a process of mutual learning and correction and enlargement and, in the end, of mutual conversion.

We do not cross the boundaries to save others, any more than we go to be saved ourselves. We do not cross boundaries to redeem other people's mistaken points of view, any more than to have our own views redeemed. We do not go to teach others, any more than we go to be taught. We do not go to communicate our message, but to discover what the message now is to be. If Western Christianity shows serious signs of exhaustion it crosses the boundaries to find nourishment and fresh springs of life.

That doesn't mean for one minute that we abandon or denigrate what we believe. What we believe is far from self-sufficient, but it is not wholly mistaken or without value. It needs others across boundaries in order to find fresh life, but it brings, with modest conviction, the life that it already has – believing that others will need what it has to bring just as it now recognizes its own need of what others have to bring. We may come to the table undernourished, but we still have food of a kind to share.

And there is another misunderstanding to clear up. Crossing boundaries does not mean finding the lowest common denom-inator that will somehow satisfy all points of view, and all religious faiths, and all the many interest groups in this plural world until the rough places become smooth. It will mean recognizing and respecting the sharp differences between us as much as welcoming agreement, and not just regretting those differences but learning from them and all the interest and stimulus they can arouse.

This crossing of boundaries as a way of life will not be easy, as many already know well. It is not a romantic solution to our troubles, as if, for example, talking to a Muslim will be any less complicated than talking to another Christian. It is a tough discipline with difficulties enough of its own. Let me mention three of them.

One has to do with power. It is all too easy for strong, established groups to shout louder than the rest. They can make themselves heard while others are not listened to, they can insist that everyone takes notice of them while others are ignored, and, despite the Internet and travel and the heady mix of our metropolitan cities, access to this very varied world is easier for some than for others. There can be no fruitful giving and receiving across boundaries if power is grossly out of balance.

A second difficulty is managing these many-sided pluralistic encounters and making them productive. We all have experience of being in touch with ever-extending networks and being involved in endless consultation but where very little gets done. At this point 'management' could well come into its own. Managing can be a tedious business especially in a church which is downsizing. It has more to do with maintenance than mission and it can be a very uninspiring occupation. But learning how to manage our encounters across the boundaries, so that they are fruitful and not frustrating, might be one of the most significant skills we need to develop on the road to tomorrow.

A third difficulty in crossing boundaries has to do with making judgments. What we encounter will never be complete. Conclusions have to be reached in a measure of ignorance. What we encounter will also be strange and the criteria we are used to may not work. We cannot be overwhelmed by what we find and we cannot dismiss it out of hand. But to accept that the postmodern world is full of highly relative points of view which need each other does not mean that all views are equally good. Clearly they are not. This is an expectant but highly critical encounter. We have to learn to discriminate and bravely make up our minds, however modestly and provisionally we learn to do so.

So we could go on. Crossing boundaries involves all sorts of problems, but cross those boundaries we must if we are to move on from the increasingly exhausted state I believe our Christianity is in. But isn't the most obvious difficulty about all this that it is all rather abstract and unreal and up in the air? It sounds a bit like those endless rounds of Faith and Order-type meetings but on a frighteningly grand scale with lots of dialogue and encounters, conversations and talks, but where, and about what, and to what end?

Seeking the common good

This brings me to a second suggestion about a Lund-type principle or rule of thumb which may help to shape our search for life. Again the suggestion isn't new. I hear it being distilled from struggle and experience and practice in many places, and it's this: if we must cross boundaries as a necessary part of everything we now do, it is not just to meet and talk with someone different, and rejuvenate our thinking and spirituality. We must cross boundaries in order to seek together the common good: the welfare of the cities, to quote the prophet, both local and global, in which we dwell.

That is not always why we cross boundaries. Too often we are tempted to cross them to seek the good of the Church; to extend the Church's boundaries; to add to its numbers; to plant it on new ground; to win for it greater understanding and support; to communicate what we already know; to underline its relevance for today; to ensure its survival and prosperity; to somehow revive its fortunes. That becomes the deep-dyed, understandable motive for so much of what we do, and which we call 'evangelism'.

We forget one part of our Christian faith that we should certainly carry with us over the boundaries for our own good and the good of all. It is there in the Old Testament in the relentless decline of Israel as Israel gets increasingly wrapped up in its own salvation. It is shot through the quirky sayings of the gospels where those who set out to save their lives are warned that they will lose them. Any institution, be it church or government or private enterprise or voluntary organization, which is purely self-seeking will in the end be self-defeating.

There is not much hope of life in crossing boundaries if all we're really up to is seeking the good of the Church. We go to seek the common good. We do not ask what can be done for the Church. We ask what can be done for humanity.

Perhaps that helps to clarify the order in which we should proceed. Perhaps we do not go in the first instance to have religious conversations or compare notes about what we do or do not believe about God and the universe, important and interesting as that at some stage may be. We go in the first instance to talk about the real-life issues of the day that concern us all. There is no shortage of them, and no shortage of women and men who want to talk about them, and no shortage of people who, if they felt they could, would want to do something about them. When the churches comment sadly that they find it difficult to make contact with 'those outside' (as they call them) they have the wrong agenda. They want to talk about the Church and religious faith when they should be talking about the common life and the welfare of the city, whether local or global: its health and education, its good governance, its hospitality to strangers, its acceptance of 'sinners', its support for the most vulnerable, its fostering of family and community. It is the easily recognizable struggle of everybody's life that is the setting for talking about our faith and the faith of all the others we begin to work with across the boundaries. Faith in the end must inspire and nourish our common endeavour. But faith is not the first or the primary topic of conversation. It is not the be-all and end-all of our encounters. We don't need Councils of Faiths so much as Alliances and Partnerships for the Common Good. Faith is to sustain and promote life. Life is not for sorting out the one true faith.

The priority of the poor

That brings me to an even more important example of how we don't abandon our Christian faith when we cross the boundaries. We take our faith with us not because we any longer harbour imperial designs or illusions of absolute grandeur, and not because we think it's the last word, but because, despite its relative nature, its ring of truth matters to us and we want to contribute it to the common quest. The belief that those who seek their own life will lose it is a part of our Christian faith we want to share. But there's a second Gospel principle that comes alive for me at this point that I want to carry with me. My attraction to it is as conditioned and relative as anything else. If I had not had the jobs I've had, and the experiences I've had, and the encounters I've had, it would never have come alive for me in quite this way. It would never have struck me as being at the heart of the Gospel. But now I'm convinced (absolutely convinced if you like) that if we want to pursue the common good and the welfare of our city then we should put the poor first: the poor to whom Jesus is said to have brought good news; the poor who are to be raised to royal status in God's kingdom, set on the thrones of the earth; the poor who are invited to the feast; the poor who are the blessed ones; the poor who are the most reliable icons of Christ in the world; the poor on whose treatment rests our whole salvation. My faith is not a trickle-down theory where you first make the rich even richer and all the boats will eventually rise. My faith is a trickle-up theory where we put the poor first and everything else will then fall into place. The priority of the poor, according to this man's incomplete and relative faith, is the key to the common good and the welfare of us all: poor and rich alike.

We know who the poor are, so we know what we cross the boundaries to do. They are the abject poor of the global city; they are the relative poor of our own cities and towns – the growing underclass of the rich world; they are the uprooted and homeless, the political and economic migrants who leave home in search of a better country; they are the marginalized, pushed out because they are sick, or single, or different; they are the victims of conflict. They are all the excluded from the mainstream who in one way or another we manage to denigrate or describe as 'sinners' in order to justify their exclusion: 'bogus' asylum seekers and 'feckless' single parents included.

As crossing boundaries becomes our way of life or discipleship there is no shortage of people for us Christians to talk to; there is no difficulty in finding things to talk about; there is no lack of things to be done for the common good; and there is no question about where to start.

Once again none of this points to an easy or romantic option where suddenly all is well, and dying churches and an exhausted Western Christian tradition suddenly find themselves swept up into dynamic alliances for change. There will be plenty of difficulties on the way. We shall come up against our own insecurities, for example. We need to let go, but we need to feel safe. There are those among us who will fear they have a lot to lose. Others may be too frail for the journey.

And we shall soon be back to the issues of power, especially if we put first the poor of the earth. Power is basically what the poor are without. Power is the engine of injustice. Power is what the powerful won't give up and it's a huge job just to even it out a bit. However, that's what has to be done in the global city and with instruments of global governance like the World Trade Organization, so that the poorer nations are properly represented and have an influential voice. That's what has to be done in our communities, so that people feel properly represented and the poorest have a say in what happens to them. Seeking the common good by putting the poorest first needs the emotional warmth of love, but in the end it cannot do without an unsentimental determination to tackle the issues of power.

And if we have to face difficult questions about power, we shall also have to face difficulties about co-option. We are called to co-operate for the common good: to be partners with governments on welfare programmes, for example; with the private sector and voluntary sectors on everything from health provision to fair trade. We have to learn again to discriminate and not simply be seduced or proselytized by all the other faiths and values we shall encounter. Co-operation and co-option are never very far apart.

Conclusion

In making my proposals in the light of the suspicion that Western Christianity is exhausted, I have not talked about the death of God, or the death of religion. I have not taken a negative view of Christianity and its potential to contribute. I have not suggested it has nothing of relevance to say. I have not suggested that all religions are much the same and in a relativist world there is little to choose between us. I have not said that anything goes. To get stuck on any of those misrepresentations is to duck the issue.

What I have done is suggest a new Lund-type principle or rule of thumb to test and shape what we do. The old one called us to act together unless conscience required us to act separately; but it called us into a togetherness that is now far too narrow and confined in a postmodern world where we see the limitations of all faith traditions and the need for them to correct and complement and nourish each other. And the old Lund Principle told us that we should act together but without specifying what the action should be. It did not take us far enough. We could be all dressed up in our unity but with nowhere to go. We need a stronger sense of direction. It has to do with crossing boundaries to seek together the common good.

The two must be firmly held together. It is no good crossing boundaries just to have interesting and in the end desultory conversations about our different faiths but without actively seeking together the common good. And it is no good seeking the welfare of the cities where we live unless we replenish each other's spiritual resources to undergird and inspire our common enterprise.

A new Lund Principle of this kind cannot be left to languish like the old one on the margins of the Church's life. It cannot be an extra-curricular activity for those who care for that sort of thing. It must fashion our core agenda: our style of life and discipleship. Crossing boundaries to seek the common good must be the benchmark of all that we do. It will affect our theological work; it will inform every aspect of mission from caring to service to evangelization; it will shape the training of ministers and lay-people, the budgets and management of our churches; and our liturgies, which are so crucial to our formation and our awareness of transcendence, cannot remain untouched.

One final remark. I think a certain kind of hope is in jeopardy. If we look at what is happening to Christianity in the Western world – at the decline of its institutions; the lessening of its influence; the dryness of its ecumenism; the impotence of its mission; its understandable turning in on itself – we may feel there is little ground for hope. Many of its people may be up to good things. Many good stories can be told, but overall we cannot buck the trend in the fortunes of the Church and the forms of Christianity that we know. Hope fades.

But that has little to do with Christian hope. The God I was taught to believe in looked out at creation and saw the darkened watery deep without form and void. It was hardly a hopeful scenario. When, as it were, God looked again, in the days of Herod the king, when Pontius Pilate was governor of Judea, and the innocents were slaughtered, and the poor still waited for their redemption, what confronted God was even less promising. As for us, faced with an unjust world and an exhausted Church, so for God: there were little grounds for hope.

Yet that is not what I understand Christian hope to be about. It does not brighten up when things apparently go well and give up when things go badly, even though such mood swings are all too human and understandable. Nor does it whistle in the dark, hoping against hope, despite the evidence.

The creative Spirit of God, moving over the face of the waters, did not bleed hope *out* of the primeval chaos. God breathed hope *in* to it. God believed in its future and, believing in it, gave it a future. The Spirit of God, quickening the child in Mary's womb, did not bleed hope out of the ugly world that went to be counted on census day. The Spirit breathed hope in. God in Christ believed in its future and so gave it a future.

Hope is not built on promising scenarios and killed off by apparently hopeless cases. Hope is believing in people and institutions and communities, in the plurality of people and communities in our postmodern world, including the communities of our churches. Hope is believing that they have a future and by believing in their future we make the future possible. Hope breeds life.

So, if we cross boundaries to seek the common good, it could well be that we shall find ourselves at that open 'table for all'[4] of which Inderjit Bhogal, a previous president of the Methodist Conference, spoke so powerfully, as long as we make sure that we are not the hosts but that everyone we find there is a joint celebrant at the feast.

That feast may indeed turn out to be a kind of wake, marking the death not just of Methodism but of Western Christianity as we know it. It does not have to be ashamed of that; it has not 'failed'; but it may have exhausted its mortal self and run its course.

We shall not, however, feast like those who indulge in drunken forgetfulness because all is lost and tomorrow we die. We shall not behave like those who have no hope. We shall eat and drink at this open 'table for all', as we have long been called to do, where the diet will be much more varied, and we shall be merry, because tomorrow we live.

---

[4] See Inderjit Bhogal, *A Table for All* (Sheffield: Penistone Publications, 2000).

2

Why Development Matters to the North

(The Churches World Development Network was in May 2001 preparing a letter to Christians worldwide explaining why development should be top of their agenda. I was asked to contribute to the arguments from the point of view of the North.)

Preliminaries

I have four preliminary points. First, I should want to be wary of writing only to Christians and fashioning arguments only for their ears. Of course, if we can mobilize all the churches in each place to side with the poor they can become a very considerable force for good. As has often been pointed out, potentially they are the biggest 'NGO' the world has ever seen. But when it comes to the so-called 'North', simply addressing Christians in our countries is not going far enough: not even as a first step. The more urgent task for Christians is not to convince themselves that development is a priority issue, but to convince the population at large. We must write a missionary manifesto, not an article for a church magazine. We can all too easily waste our time trying to overcome the churches' resistance to development and never get to the really strategic task of overcoming the world's resistance. In any case, Christians in the North are not so very different from all the other people in the North when it comes to persuading them to act in these matters. The arguments that are likely to impress the one are just as likely to impress the other: and those surely are the arguments we are looking for. They are not just high-sounding, idealistic arguments, but strategic arguments that are actually effective in moving the whole development process along, winning as much active support as possible. Our arguments should be informed and inspired by the best in our Christian faith, but they should not be fashioned for Christian ears alone, or appeal too narrowly on Christian grounds.

Second, we shall make a big mistake if we write to people, Christian or otherwise, as if they were isolated individuals or members of a homogeneous group. The North is complex and varied. Its peoples are members of social classes and ethnic groups. They owe allegiance to political parties. They join voluntary organizations. They are members of the electorate once characterized by J. K. Galbraith among others as 'the comfortable majority' with 'a growing underclass'. They work in manufacturing and service industries, many of which are linked to transnational corporations. They run the social security system or look to it for support. They sit in parliaments or run the governments of the North with more than one eye over their shoulders, wondering what the electorate will want of them next. And altogether they are members of nation states. These are the real addressees to whom our letter must be posted. These are the varied human realities, corporate as well as individual, large scale as well as small scale, formal as well as friendly, that we have to persuade and activate for good. Their interests and motivations are not always the same. The arguments that appeal to one group may not necessarily appeal to another. Individuals, including Christian individuals, can be pulled in different directions since they live in more than one reality: when they sit in church, for example, they can be pulled one way, and when they go to work in the city or to shop in the supermarket, or even to vote in an election, they can be pulled in another.

A third preliminary point has less to do with who we are talking to and more to do with what we are talking about. The programme for the Churches World Development Network meeting at High Leigh in England uses two phrases. It talks about 'eradicating poverty' and it talks about 'world development'. They're not necessarily the same. I prefer the first to the second. 'Development' as a word is getting tired. It is not very energizing. It is hard to divorce from the North–South scenario perpetuated in the language of the conference and no longer very satisfactory either. It is hard again to widen the concept of 'development' beyond economic development and economic growth; and economic development and growth, as we all know, can militate against the interests of the poor as well as work in their favour, or be made to work in their favour according to a UK government White Paper published in 2000.[1]

But even the phrase 'eradicating poverty' begs a lot of questions. Are we talking about 'absolute' poverty, which we might eradicate, or 'relative' poverty, which we will never eradicate? Does it include 'material', 'cultural' and 'spiritual' poverty? Even if we're clear about what we want to achieve, we are still left with all the crucial questions about how best to achieve it, from 'aid' to structural change. Agreeing about that and winning support for it may be a tougher and even more important task politically than winning support for the overall aim.

A fourth point was raised by a Colloquium in Delhi in November 2000.[2] It was made up largely of representatives of the so-called 'South' or poorer countries. They insisted that 'wealth' was as much of an issue for them as 'poverty'. They wanted to eradicate poverty, of course, but they also wanted to eradicate 'excessive wealth' and 'greed' and to put in their place what they began to call 'holistic wealth', which would incorporate the spiritual and cultural as well as the material in an attractive, sustainable and rounded way of life. In other words, they wanted to win support for eradicating not only the poverty of their deprivation but what they regarded as the poverty of our excess.

In the light of these preliminary remarks I want to think about what we should write not to the Christians of the North but to the varied peoples of the North about why poverty eradication is one of the most important things for them to think about today.

Self-interest

The more astute will almost certainly reach immediately for the argument about *self-interest.* You meet it straight away in the British government's White Paper on Development – *Eliminating World*

---

[1] *Eliminating World Poverty: Making Globalisation Work for the Poor* (London: HMSO, 2000).

[2] See Michael Taylor, *Christianity, Poverty and Wealth* (London: SPCK; Geneva: WCC, 2003), pp. 83–4.

Poverty: Making Globalisation Work for the Poor. It is referred to in the foreword by Tony Blair. He recognizes the strong moral arguments but quickly adds that eliminating world poverty 'is also in the UK's national interest'.[3] It is a perfectly acceptable line of argument for Christians to pursue. The law of Christ is summed up in the injunction to love God and to love our neighbour as ourselves. Self-love may not be enough but it is certainly not ruled out.

Christian Realism actually requires us to rule it in. The Christian analysis of our human nature points to a creative and generous side to our personalities, made as we say in the image of God, but to a much darker side as well, which we label 'fallen' or 'sinful'. In my judgment it is less the result of our wilful disobedience and disregard for God's will and has more to do with our deep-seated insecurity, often physical (as in the case of material poverty) but also psychological and spiritual, even 'existential', in this earthly environment where what we don't know about our existence far outweighs what we do. This insecurity leads us to be highly defensive and watchful for our own safety. The result is the destructive egotism that lies at the root of so much of the world's conflicts, large and small. Whenever we are in a position to do so, we take the decisions that we believe are most likely to favour us. We use what power we have to look after ourselves. We ignore or override or disadvantage those who are weaker than us and cannot stand up for themselves. Although it is not the whole story, for much of the time we are motivated by self-interest.

If that is true of us as individuals, it is even more the case when we gather into groups and social classes; and it is quite overtly the case when it comes, say, to a large business concern or the nation state. A business exists to make profits and serve the interests of its shareholders. It serves the public only to the extent that, if it is of no use to people and meets none of their demands in the market place, then it will quickly go to the wall. The nation state and its government exist almost by definition to serve the national interest. If, for example, Tony Blair and his ministers did not look out first and foremost for Britain in world and European affairs, then they would not be doing their job.

Christians and their churches have a tendency to appeal only to our better natures. They challenge us to think of others and to be

[3] *Eliminating World Poverty*, p. 6

generous and kind and fair. They should not be surprised when for much of the time the response is disappointing. If they are disappointed then Christians can be criticized for naivety and for ignoring their own Christian teaching. They are not dealing with human beings as they really are. If we are serious about changing the world, including global capitalism, in favour of the poor, then we shall opt for an effective strategy of persuasion, not just a high-sounding one. We shall hammer home the point whenever we can that eradicating poverty is in everybody's interest including ours, and not just in the interests of the world's poor.

Here are four familiar arguments. First comes the economic argument. Once the poorer countries are integrated into the global economy it will be better for everyone. It will increase the volume of profitable world trade. Once tariffs are lowered or done away with altogether the poor will have more to sell at competitive prices. Once their own markets are open to us we shall be able to exploit them and sell our goods and services to them. It is not a zero-sum game where the poor will only prosper at the expense of the rich. All the boats will rise.

A second argument recognizes the link between poverty and conflict. They aggravate and reinforce one another. Taken together they not only produce problems for Africa or Latin America, for example, but for the rest of us. The illicit drugs trade is one of them and migration is seen as another. We talk of 'bogus asylum seekers' but these are often men and women fleeing from poverty and economic misery just as much as from terror and violence. They are looking for work and a better life as well as safety. They do not abandon home and country just for the sake of it. Deal with the problem back home, however, and support development, and the problem for the rest of us will begin to go away too.

A third argument concerns the environment. Poverty and conflict both contribute to the destruction of the environment which in turn contributes to global warming which in turn is a threat to us all.

Fourth comes a vaguer and more philosophical argument which was, however, articulated more than once in the reports and discussions following the anti-capitalist demonstrations in London, England on May Day 2001. It touches on the concept of 'holistic wealth' which I referred to above. Our present way of life in the one-third rich world not only consigns many of our fellow human beings to poverty, it is also unsustainable and at the end of the day it does not make us all that happy. Tackling world poverty will require us to change our style of life but, far from leaving us with a sense of deprivation and having to go without, and far from 'impoverishing' us as consumers, the end result will actually be more satisfying and enjoyable. Our quality of life in a world where poverty has been radically reduced will be positively enhanced.

So, a persuasive letter to the peoples of the so-called 'North' must make clear that what we are urging upon them is in their own self-interest. Poverty eradication is good for the rich. It's good for 'us'! This important line of argument has, however, its own difficulties. Here are two of them.

Difficulties

First, it is not entirely clear or predictable that measures that benefit the world's poorest will necessarily benefit us. If we are serious about health and education for all in the South then, for example, we should probably stop filling the gaps in our own health and education services by cherry-picking teachers and doctors and nurses from the South. If we want an end to speculative capital flows that do nothing for investment in poor countries and a great deal for the capital gains of the rich, then presumably we should agree to less returns on our own investments. If we want fair trade we may have to pay higher prices. If we want to reduce conflict then profits from the sale of arms and jobs in the arms manufacturing industry will be at risk. If we want sustainability and an end to global warming we shall have to get out of our cars, as it were, and get on our bikes. And so we could go on.

But there is a much more all-embracing scenario which suggests that the necessary changes may not be to the obvious advantage of the likes of us. Let me remind you of what I regard, a priori, as the most fundamental strategy if we are out to combat poverty and reduce the growing gap between the excessively rich and the poor. It is the age-old strategy of empowerment. Earlier we noted that the darker side of human nature leads us, when we have the power to do so, to take decisions which are in our own favour and against the interests of the weak and the poor. We do it as individuals, as social groups, as banks and corporations, as nations and communities of nations. This exercise of power against the poor and the weak runs through the history of colonization with its accompanying exploitation, and it still characterizes the global economy and market place. International debt, looked at from one perspective, adds up to a puny amount of money compared with global financial transactions. Why then is it not cancelled and done away with? Because it is an instrument of control. It is but one more example of the strong exercising their power over the weak, bending them to the will of the well-off and leaving the disadvantaged without medicines, hospitals and schools in the process.

This imbalance of power is one of the most critical engines of injustice. The way to tackle that injustice is not, of course, to reverse power (as the Magnificat suggests by bringing down the mighty and lifting up those of low degree) since once the weak become strong they behave like the strong. No, the way to tackle it is to work towards a better balance of power so that peoples and countries with different interests can stand up to each other on more equal terms. The strategy is to ensure that no bullies can have their way in any of the playgrounds of the world, whether political, economic, cultural or religious.

What does this strategy mean in practice when it comes to the global economy? What does it mean when we come, in the language, for example, of the UK's Department for International Development, to 'making globalization work for the poor'? There are two parts to the answer.

First, the so-called 'free market' (never of course free for all) must be brought under control. Markets can be effective and 'human' mechanisms for the exchange of goods and services to everyone's benefit. Country markets and farmers' markets all over the world are evidence of that. But markets must be contained within a firm social context. They must be 'social markets' where instruments of governance – national, international and global – reach the issues that markets left to themselves will never reach. They must ensure, for example, that everyone has a fair chance to trade; that the benefits of trade are distributed fairly; that what is earned in the market place contributes to what will never be adequately taken care of by market forces, including education and healthcare for everyone and the infrastructures that make markets accessible.

But, second, these instruments of governance must not fall solely into the hands of a few, or else, once again, under cover of a thin veil of legitimacy (as Marx astutely observed), the strong are overpowering and exploiting the weak. What masquerade as objective laws turn out to be little more than ways of protecting the interests of the few. Governance, therefore, has to be along democratic lines. The concept of democracy, like any other, can be misused and is not easily transplanted from one culture to another but, properly understood, democracy (or perhaps better 'participation') ensures that everyone has a say in decision-making and no one is left unchecked to act forever only for their own advantage.

In practical terms, this strategy of empowerment, applied to the global market place, means the creation or reform of instruments of global governance so that they are run on democratic lines. The World Trade Organization is the most frequently targeted example at the moment. It is undemocratic because poorer countries cannot afford to be properly represented and it therefore makes rules to suit the rich. Poorer countries cannot fully participate. Their people cannot come or, if they do come, they do not have access to the kind of briefings or back-up that would make their participation influential. Promoting global governance through the World Trade Organization, the international financial institutions and through a reformed United Nations, all run on democratic principles, is one of the more important agenda items for those committed to the eradication of poverty.

Yet it is almost a matter of commonsense to recognize that if we are successful in all of this the result will not be an obvious victory for the interests of the powerful. It is not necessarily to their advantage. Their power to roam the world freely and use the world's resources and peoples as they will, will be severely tamed. We may mount subtle arguments to suggest that in the long run we shall all be the winners, but the immediate outcome ought to be that the poor, given a greater chance to rule the world and look after their own interests, will benefit more than the rich. On the debt front, for example, we should certainly no longer be in a position to demand our pound of flesh.

Which brings us to a second difficulty about the argument from self-interest. Most arguments about the self-interest of the rich, designed to persuade them to go along with policies that will reduce or eradicate poverty, are about their long-term rather than short-term self-interest, or about their 'enlightened self-interest' or the 'common interest' of us all. In other words they are not about immediate benefits, which means they don't exactly or easily appeal to a society which is not looking for bread for tomorrow but bread for today. The kind of lifestyle that most people have been led to believe they want and will make them happy, in other words, the lifestyle they are 'interested' in, is of a more instant variety. It is about quick returns. It is as immediate as a lottery prize or a low-priced consumer bonanza rather than a more distant concept of a safer and happier world and a more holistic life for their grandchildren.

'Enlightened self-interest' is not the easiest of interests to appeal to. The environment and what many are convinced is looming global disaster is a worrying example. The evidence of global warming is everywhere to see, from rising sea levels, to storm and tempest, to disastrous floods affecting not just the South but the North. It is in everybody's interest to stop it and stop it now. But efforts to do so are spectacularly turned aside. Radical changes in transport policy seem to get nowhere fast. President Bush would have nothing to do with Kyoto and its over-modest proposals – and not because they were modest. Even here, in the face of an obvious threat, the appeal to self-interest seems ineffective. The edge of it is blunted by more powerful interests like those of the oil-producing companies of Bush's USA; and no doubt by the fact that rich countries have the money to defend themselves from disaster in ways that poor countries do not. The lesson we need to draw, in deciding what to say to our fellow citizens in the North, is that the self-interest we appeal to is usually 'enlightened' or 'long-term' self-interest and that this will always have a hard time pressing its case compared to the interests that are immediately to hand and to policies that promise more immediate delivery.

One last point should be noted. Peoples of the North are not homogeneous. Their interests are not always the same. Until recently, for example, voluntary organizations working with the world's poor saw the private sector as an implacable enemy, and the relationship remains uneasy. Their interests do not entirely coincide. To mount an argument which appeals to the shared or common self-interest of the North will require an uphill struggle when faced with the competing and conflicting or changing interests of those we set out to persuade. It may also require us to address different constituencies in rather different ways.

The moral arguments

I have suggested that writing to the peoples of the North to encourage them to support the struggle to eliminate world poverty on the grounds that it is in their interests to do so is an important Christian line of argument, but it may not be as easy or straightforward or effective as Christian realists like me may like to think.

What, then, about the *moral* arguments for supporting the struggle against poverty? Taken by themselves, moral arguments will not be sufficiently persuasive. The darker, self-centred side to our human nature is good at turning a deaf ear. But that does not mean that moral arguments have no power to persuade at all, and it certainly does not mean that they can be ignored.

First, a reminder of what they are and what they are not! They are definitely not about who deserves what. The poor, especially the 'deserving' poor, ought to have more, while the rich ought to have less. This kind of argument has more to do with romanticizing about the poor than with morality. The real difference between rich and poor has nothing to do with their moral qualities, including their just deserts. We readily agree, although many of our fellow citizens in the North do not, that the poor are not poor because they are generally lazy and irresponsible (as well as slow-witted) any more than the rich are rich because they are all hard workers who face up to their responsibilities as parents and citizens (as well as being gifted and intelligent). That kind of misrepresentation, not to say racism, needs to be constantly exposed and nailed wherever we find it. It is equally untrue (even though the Bible with its links between the 'poor' and the 'godly' appears to support it from time to time) that the poor represent the 'goodies' who deserve a better deal in life, while the rich represent the 'baddies' who ought to be brought down a peg or two. That is a kind of reverse racism or prejudice. The fact is that there are no differences between rich and poor. Rich people, as well as poor people, can be idle and far too dependent on others. Poor people, as well as rich people, can be irresponsible and exploitative. Both rich and poor are, generally speaking, prepared to work hard and much prefer to be fairly independent and earn their own living rather than be recipients of other people's charity.

The real difference between rich and poor is that the rich have the opportunities to make their own way in the world and exercise their talents productively, whereas the poor do not. There is no denying that from time to time we can rightly differentiate between certain people who deserve more or less than others because of what they have done; but that can be a difference between two rich people or between two poor people as well as between a rich and a poor person. It is not, however, the difference between rich and poor as such, and the moral case for eradicating poverty has nothing to do with our deserts.

We could no doubt argue for a long time about what precisely it does have to do with. The big word for most activists is 'justice' or 'fairness'. The struggle to eliminate poverty is important to the North because it's a moral struggle for justice or a fairer world. If we are asked what that means in practice, two obvious answers come to mind.

First, justice demands that everyone receives a fair return for the work they do and the contribution they make to the inter-dependent web of our common life. On any reckoning, that is manifestly not the case today. It is certainly not the case, for example, in relation to women, least of all poor women. They make an immense contribution to the domestic economy. They fetch water; they work in the fields; they wash and clean and cook; they bear children and care for them; they make and mend. Much of this work goes unrecognized and unrecorded in monetary terms and is left out of most economic reckonings. Millions of poor people, women included, work as hard if not harder than any workaholic in the North, but the returns by comparison are negligible. In one place hard work spells comfort; in another place hard work reaps little but destitution. This is one of the mainsprings of fair trade campaigns: to ensure through codes of good practice, implemented and monitored, that Third World producers get better prices for their products and Third World workers get better working conditions and a decent wage. That, in practice, is what we mean by 'justice'.

Of course, as always, it is more complicated than it sounds. People work in different ways and make different contributions. Some work with their hands. Some are more skilled or differently skilled than others. Some contribute ideas. In the rich North some contribute their financial assets or work at buying and selling and moving money about. Some of these contributions are valued more highly than others; some are scarcer than others, and the rewards they enjoy can vary greatly in a competitive market place. Deciding what is a 'fair' return for work done is not a simple matter; which is one reason why those in the North who seek after justice will be attracted to the concept of a 'minimum wage' and why those who seek after justice for the poor of the earth will be attracted to the concepts of 'sustainable livelihoods' and 'entitlements', by which a man or woman receives at least enough for them and their dependants to maintain their lives in a sustainable way. Short of justice we must maintain this bottom line.

Second, in practice justice demands that everyone not only receives a fair return for their work but a fair share of the available resources and opportunities which allow people to work and use their labour and skills and intellects productively. This is the aspect of justice which is often referred to these days as 'inclusion' as opposed to 'exclusion'. It is unjust that some can exploit the benefits of the market place while others cannot. It is unjust that some have access to huge tracts of land while others have access to none. It is unjust that some benefit from advanced information technology while others do not. It is unjust that some receive education and healthcare, gaining the health and knowledge that enable them to prosper, while others are left without schools and medicine. Some of these basic issues are addressed in the United Nations Millennium Development Goals for 2015; others are reflected in the battles over World Trade Organization-inspired rules and regulations governing the market place.

There are other important areas of moral argument besides the basic claims of justice. One has to do with the environment and its fragile, inter-related structure and limited resources. There are intimate links between environmental and poverty issues. Disregard for the environment produces poverty. Poverty destroys the environment. We have a moral duty to take care of the earth and its ability to support life. We must manage its resources wisely. We must ensure that they are used in sustainable ways and passed on in a fit state to future generations. We should not exploit the earth but exercise stewardship of the so-called 'natural order'. That does not forbid us to interfere with it as is sometimes

implied, but it does require us to do so with understanding and respect.

The argument about justice and fairness, however, probably remains the most compelling moral reason why the North should put poverty eradication high on its agenda. A world where the by now familiar statistical pictures of gross inequality are still all too true – where 25 per cent of us enjoy and use up 75 per cent of the earth's resources and 25 per cent enjoy scarcely any of those resources at all (and are still accused of having too many children and putting an unacceptable strain on the environment) – is morally indefensible. We ought to reduce the still-widening gap.

Difficulties

There are, however, difficulties in appealing to people on moral grounds, just as there are in appealing to self-interest, besides the fact that most of us are good at turning a deaf ear. For example, in the end moral values have their roots in what we believe about our world and ourselves, and those beliefs are often religious beliefs. 'What ought to be' – the moral claim on us all – is rooted in 'what is the case' or what we believe to be the nature of the reality we are dealing with. If you insist on moral grounds that any interference with the reproductive process by using contraception is wrong and you are asked why, you will in the end come up with your belief that sexual relations are about having children. That is their nature. That is what they were designed for. That is why God made us in a particular way. So that is how they should be used. A moral 'ought' is rooted in a believing 'is'. If you say children ought to be educated, it is because you believe that they are made for growth and personal development. The 'ought' is rooted in an 'is'.

The same is true when we insist on justice. Why do we believe that everyone should have a fair chance and a fair share of the earth's resources? If we are pressed as Christians on these points we shall probably come up with three kinds of answer. One is that we believe that the earth and its resources were not created by God to be the objects of a smash-and-grab raid by a minority of powerful colonialists and empire builders who could then enjoy most of them at the expense of the rest. Rather, we believe the earth and its resources were made by God to sustain all of us and for all of us to share. A second answer is that as human beings there may be advantages in enjoying a bit of healthy competition between us from time to time but that we are made primarily not to compete but to co-operate. Yet a third answer is that we believe God has not made all of us the same but that God does regard all of us as equally important and worthy of respect, and with a shared destiny to grow up and flourish until we reach the full stature of the children of God. The means to do so should therefore be equally available to us all. The 'ought' of justice when pressed to explain itself is forced to issue creedal statements about what we believe to be the case about ourselves and our world.

We can therefore see why there are difficulties about moral appeals besides the fact that they are easily ignored. One is that, if religious belief fades, the morality which grows out of it may lose its grip; and there is some evidence in the debate about secularization, for example, that this is the case. Alasdair MacIntyre's outstanding analysis of contemporary Western culture in *After Virtue* has a good deal to say about all of that.[4]

Second, if moral claims are rooted in religious beliefs, where religious beliefs differ, as they do in our increasingly multi-faith Northern societies, then the morality which grows out of them may differ as well. Once again we may have to appeal to different constituencies with rather different arguments. Each one may believe its own moral values are universal and apply equally to everyone across the board, but these universal values may not always be the same. Different beliefs, even within Christianity, can throw up very different attitudes to the poor.

Moral appeals may not, therefore, be quite so universal or straightforward as they appear. Justice and fairness may not resonate across the board. Is there good reason, nevertheless, to think there is significant common moral ground between very different groups? 'Human rights', for example, have become an increasingly important concept for development over recent years. The concept of 'rights' has been widened to include livelihoods, education and clean water as well as political freedom. Development targets which can be met as and when resources become available have been turned into 'legal' requirements, which governments must face up to today rather than tomorrow. Education for all is not merely a desirable goal but a right to be claimed and a duty to be done as of now. Human rights can also

---

[4] Alasdair MacIntyre, *After Virtue* (London: Duckworth Press, 1984).

be pressed into service in our attempts to persuade the peoples of the North to put the eradication of poverty high on their agenda. We can appeal to them because it's a matter of 'human rights'. The language is familiar since human rights legislation is now much talked about, for instance under European law, and most people are used to talking about their own rights if not the rights of others; and human rights are regarded as universal. We talk, for example, about the 'Universal Declaration of Human Rights'. They apply to everyone of whatever race or creed; and they combine in an interesting way the language of morality and the language of faith. There may well, therefore, be beliefs about all human beings that are shared by all human beings and that suggest that all human beings have similar moral obligations to each other. 'Human rights' may be the substance of the 'global ethic' of the future.

But there is still room for caution. Some see human rights as too individualistic a concept and far too Western in character. Even where the language is shared, the content, such as the rights of women, may be different. And global ethics can obscure the distinctiveness of faith traditions where the differences can be more interesting and illuminating than the similarities. Co-operation in development is essential and there can be little of it without a sense of common ground. The search for it, however, may be just as fruitful by way of dialogue between very different faith communities in the hope of discovering ways forward together[5] as by way of establishing global agreements on ethics and rights.

Compassion and vision

Finally, two other types of argument should be considered when we set out to persuade the peoples of the North to take poverty eradication seriously. Both have strong links with our Christian faith.

One might be called 'humanitarian'. I hesitate to use the word because it is in danger itself of sounding less than human. The phrase 'humanitarian aid', for example, conjures up for me these days pictures of highly competitive fundraising, big money and big

[5] One of the aims of the World Faiths Development Dialogue.

business, large-scale operations, huge disaster scenarios, press and profile battles between agencies in which the human can all too easily get lost. If we are to appeal for action on humanitarian grounds, of course we need to convey the scale of the problem, but we also need to get beyond the statistics to the highly individual people involved and, while being clear about our moral obligations, we also need to get beyond our duties and cold morality to a warmer fellow-feeling which might be better called not 'sentiment' but 'compassion'. We need to touch the hearts of people, not just their consciences or their hard-headedness or self-interest. It is here that pictures and stories and the voices of the poor may prove more compelling than logic and arguments. Personally I can feel the force of a moral claim and I can be pulled by self-interest, but my motivation is more often renewed by returning in memory and the mind's eye to what I call 'the icons of the poor': the unique but representative faces of so many – the cameo portraits, for example, of a mother in a refugee camp in Zaire cradling her child at her dry breast; or a desperate father and farmer in the Horn of Africa defiantly sowing his seeds again and again in the face of drought; or two bright young people in the rain forests of Brazil enjoying a way of life which the loggers threaten to take away in the name of 'development'.

A further line of approach has to do with vision. If we need to appeal to the head (self-interest) and the conscience (morality) and the heart (compassion) we need to appeal to the imagination in ways that lift the spirit and generate enthusiasm. We need the poetry as well as the prose. We need to evoke pictures of a better world: where everyone can flourish; where very different people live together in mutual respect, co-operation and peace; where nature sustains and is sustained; where there is education and healthcare for all; where everyone has a chance to use their talents productively; where people hunger and thirst no more and there is bread for all and energy to dance and play. We need to set before an often jaded population in the North the vision of a new heaven and a new earth. I doubt that any great movement in history, from Marxism to Socialism to Western capitalism, would have gained ground without it. Christianity certainly has not. It cries out with the Old Testament prophets for justice in the gate of the city but at the same time it raises our eyes in the Book of Revelation to the vision of the city of God, which comes down from heaven like a bride adorned for her husband.

Yet visions, if they are not to evaporate into mere utopias, need some substance in at least two respects. One is the reassurance that there are some viable and attractive alternatives in the middle distance to the world as we know it; that our talk of a different world is not just an idle dream; that we have positive proposals to make as well as negative criticisms. The debate about alternative internal, or localized, economies is an interesting and encouraging example. There is no suggestion that we can remove ourselves entirely from the global economy which on the one hand does little for the poor while on the other, so we are told, is their only hope once they have learned its ways. To put it differently, none of us can entirely free ourselves from the influences of the big outside world, its trading patterns and market places. None of us can be completely independent of it and if we try to be we should probably be the losers in the long run. But localized economies can put people in a better position to resist some of the unwelcome pressures of the global economy and make their own decisions. Such economies, whether very local (urban or rural), regional or national, or covering a much larger sub-continental area, will try to make the best use of their own resources, buying and selling local goods and using local skills and services to meet their needs. An internalized economy will be biased towards using what is near to hand before reaching out for it across the globe. It can be more environmentally friendly and use resources in a more sustainable way. It can offer local people opportunities to earn a living. It can balance out the power between the local and the global. It can potentially be more participatory and democratic and give a greater sense of control.

How local economies can successfully interact and support each other, avoiding disparities between islands of plenty where internal resources are in good supply and islands of scarcity where they are not, remains a largely unresolved question to date, but 'localization' and proposals like it help to build the necessary bridges of credibility between the visions of the New World, which generate greater enthusiasm but can seem to be too good and too far off to be true, and the harsh reality of the present world which seems difficult to change and about which it is all too easy to sigh and say with the Thatcherites and capitalist triumphalists: There Is No Alternative (TINA).

Second, our vision needs to be backed by the reassurance that 'ordinary' men and women are not powerless to change things. In

2001, the slogan for Christian Aid Week was: 'You can make a difference.' It could be misused to hide the fact that the struggle against poverty is difficult and often disappointing, requiring patience and persistence and only won at considerable cost. It could become a misleading and sentimental slogan, kidding people that a £1 coin in a red envelope is all that the Lord requires of them to change the world. But people say they feel powerless. In the face of growing injustice, a global economy that seems difficult to divert from its path, and multinationals apparently a law unto themselves, they wonder if there is anything they can do. At which point they need reassuring that visions are not just impossible dreams and that we *can* make a difference. On 16 May 1998, up to 70,000 'ordinary' people ring-fenced the G8 Summit Meeting in Birmingham, UK and put the issue of international debt firmly on its agenda and on the agendas of the World Bank and the International Monetary Fund. Today a large part of that debt is still uncancelled and a scandal remains, but those people did make a difference, as a result of which some children who would never have had an education and might never have survived at all are going to school.

There is a limit to how far the North will be motivated by moral appeals or appeals to self-interest. They need something other than this relatively dry dust. They need an attractive vision as long as we give it substance by offering real alternatives and reassuring evidence that they have the power to bring about change.

Conclusion

Why does development matter to the North? I have suggested three main lines of argument. One has to do with self-interest; a second has to do with morality; a third has to do with affairs of the heart and of the spirit: with compassion and vision.

I have hedged all my arguments about with hesitations. Self-interest: because strengthening the poor may not be such a benefit for the rich or even as harmless to their cause as we may be tempted to make out. Morality: because a cry for justice, even an appeal to a sense of 'fair play', may well fall on deaf ears or be more complicated than we might think in a multi-faith society on the one hand and a secular society on the other. Appeals to the heart can dissolve into sentiment; and visions can evaporate into utopian dreams.

So there are qualifications all round. The trumpet gives an uncertain sound. That is not necessarily the case at all. Nothing is to be gained by ignoring the difficulties of any task, whether it is tackling poverty or motivating the North to put poverty eradication high on its agenda. Indeed, when we are open and honest with people about the difficulties, rather than covering them up or patronizing our listeners in case they can't cope, they are often energized and 'turned on' rather than 'turned off'. Difficulties and complexities are not necessarily demotivating any more than they are reasons for doing and saying nothing. Understanding them provides the necessary wisdom for doing a better job, not an excuse for abandoning the job altogether. Maturity, including Christian maturity, has nothing to do with pretending the shadows don't exist. Christian maturity involves the frank recognition that the world does not offer tremendous grounds for hope either to us or to God; but, like God, we choose to hope in its future nevertheless. Christian maturity involves us in recognizing that all arguments and points of view are relative rather than absolute: that all have their serious limitations; while still taking our courage in both hands and being thoroughly committed to what seems best to us for the time being. Christian maturity involves us in recognizing that this is not a simple, straightforward world but a complex one, full of 'ifs' and 'buts'; but recognizing, nevertheless that our humanity lies in taking firm responsibility and, for all the complexities, being decisive. Christian maturity means acting and speaking with conviction while at the same time practising the humility that knows we can never be wholly right. We may tremble in our shoes but we shall sound the trumpet for all that.

If I wrote a letter about development to the peoples of the North I would probably do so along the following lines:

- I would try to keep the varied recipients and their interests very clearly in mind.
- I would try to persuade them to support the struggle against poverty through aid, development projects, support of Third World civil society, the reform of the global economic institutions and their policies, the establishment of global

governance based on international law, and through courts of justice based on human rights.

- I would make clear that I argue out of my Christian faith because it is important for me, without claiming it as the only or sufficient source of wisdom.
- I would not hide the difficulties but still make my case as clearly and passionately as I could.
- I would argue on four main grounds.

First, on compassionate grounds, telling highly personal stories that touch the heart.

Second, on moral grounds, doing my best to thunder at length like an Old Testament prophet, showing all the righteous (I hope not self-righteous) anger I can muster in the face of injustice and illustrating it time and again.

Third, appealing to self-interest, I would not insist too much on the clear cut advantages for the rich if we eradicate poverty, but I would try to put the fear of God into people by highlighting the growing dangers for all of us if we do nothing about poverty and injustice.

Finally, I would profess my belief that an alternative fairer world is not only a possibility but an attractive prospect for all of us: where our riches are no longer excessive or exploitative but shared; where the desert flowers in due season; where the enemy looks more like a friend; and where the poor of the earth no longer constitute a threat or a burden of guilt but become our neighbours whose company and colleagueship we enjoy.

But, of course, my words will carry little weight unless they are made flesh and what I do suggests I believe what I say.

3

Facing Up to Reality:
The Future of the Poor[1]

Different realities

'Facing Up to Reality' invites a number of questions and comments about reality itself: is 'reality' necessarily rather grim – as being challenged to face up to it suggests; whose reality are we talking about and can we talk about it any longer in an objective sense; isn't the only postmodern 'reality' the end of reality; and in what sense does theology help us to understand reality better and deal with it more effectively? To some of these questions we shall return, if only indirectly, but let me begin in a reasonably straightforward, descriptive way.

The year 2002 saw the completion of a five-year study programme in 24 countries, most but not all of them poor and in the South: countries such as Ghana, Namibia, Bangladesh, Fiji, Colombia and Nicaragua.[2] It was funded by the ecumenical aid and development agencies in Europe, such as Christian Aid in the UK and Bread for the World in Germany. These organizations, and their ways of working, grew up in the second half of the twentieth century. Many of them were set up together with the Bretton Woods institutions in the aftermath of the Second World War. Those were the days when no one talked of globalization; when everyone talked about the Cold War and the East/West

---

[1] A lecture to the Manchester Theological Society (UK) in February 2002. 'Facing Up to Reality' was the general title of a series of lectures organised by the Society.

[2] See Taylor, *Christianity, Poverty and Wealth*.

divide, and when the language of North and South seemed a reasonably accurate way to refer to the richer and the poorer parts of the earth. Since then all that has changed and much else, and the turn of the new millennium seemed a good moment to ask whether the way the churches and their agencies respond to world poverty should be different and, if so, how.

The enquiry was pursued by a series of case studies in the 24 countries. In each one the same questions were asked of the same groups of people as far as widely differing circumstances allowed. Rich and poor communities, government officials, economists and industrialists, church leaders and NGOs were all asked about poverty: its nature and its causes, whether it was advancing or in retreat, what the churches taught about it and what the churches and their agencies were doing and should now be doing, along with many others of course, to eliminate it.

The results of the study are not startling but they are interesting. Among its findings there is a fairly widely shared view of what might be called 'the reality we face'. Poverty does not go away. If there is a percentage-wise improvement in some countries, overall the numbers of the poor increase as does the gap between rich and poor both between and within countries. On one point there is virtual unanimity, including a highly developed country like Germany, and that is that the global economic system and the economic policies pursued by the G8, the World Bank, the International Monetary Fund (IMF) and the World Trade Organization (WTO) are no friends of the poor. In general they are seen and judged as doing the poor more harm than good. On this particular point they join, at least in spirit, the anti-globalization movement as it mobilized round the world from Seattle to Genoa and, in early February 2002, in New York.

I hardly need to point out that the unanimous view of these 24 case studies is not the only view of reality. Statistics can be quoted from the development reports of the United Nations (UN), the World Bank and others, which paint a more promising picture. Some of the poverty indicators move in the right direction: more children go to school; fewer babies die; more families have clean water to drink; average per capita incomes improve despite the one billion and more who are routinely said to live on less than a dollar a day. 'Things are looking up,' as they say, in the Third World. This alternative view also believes it knows the reason why, and not always with the zeal of neo-liberal fundamentalists. The way out of poverty is the wealth that the global economy can and does create. Among the mechanisms it successfully employs to do so is an increasingly free flow of trade across the world. If the poor countries are sensible and brave enough (since at first the waters can be chilly) to dip their toes in and then learn to swim with the tide, they will surely benefit, and there are statistics to prove that this is true. No one denies that the global economy needs adapting and reforming. It is certainly not perfect; but when it comes down to it this global, capitalist system is the best. Historically, it has brought whole countries and continents out of poverty. Looking to the future, some would say it is the only hope of the poor: 'There is no alternative'.

A recent paper by a senior commentator within the World Bank recognizes these differing accounts of reality.[3] They were brought home to her by the Jubilee 2000 Campaign and again at a Colloquium she attended in June 2001:

> The Colloquium confronted two radically different views of globalisation (with numerous perspectives in between). At one extreme was a profoundly pessimistic view of a world whose spirit, culture and physical environment are on a rapidly descending slope. Globalisation was repeatedly described as a predatory phenomenon, by one participant as a vampire. At the other extreme was the view of globalisation as a complex, unstoppable force bringing opportunity for most of the world's people, even though it also posed 'downside' problems and challenges which can and must be managed.... As is often the case in discussions of globalisation, individuals bring very different perspectives and values, but also a contrasting and often contradictory array of facts. In this setting, where the range of disciplines, nationalities, and experience were so broad, it was still more apparent how very widely the pictures of reality differed.[4]

---

[3] Katherine Marshall, 'Development and Religion: a Different Lens on Development Debates', (Washington: World Bank, 2002).

[4] Marshall, 'Development and Religion', pp. 17–18.

Why we differ

An article by Ravi Kanbur is even more interesting.[5] He was Director of the World Bank's *World Development Report on Poverty* until outside pressures on him, trying to dictate what the Report should and should not say, led him to resign in May 2000. Ravi Kanbur recognizes disagreements over whether world poverty is on the increase or in decline, so that when, for example, World Bank officials produced carefully researched and adjusted figures showing that poverty had gone down in Ghana, very few people 'from academics in the universities, through foreign and local NGOs, to the trade unions and the Rotary Clubs' believed them. There was in fact 'an astonishing degree of disbelief'. Ravi Kanbur characterizes the disagreements and divisions over whether or not existing economic policies are likely to benefit the poor. On the one hand 'are those (referred to as Group A types) who tend to believe that the cause of poverty reduction is best served by more rapid adjustment to fiscal imbalances, rapid adjustment to lower inflation and external deficits and the use of high interest rates to achieve these ends, internal and external financial sector liberal- isation, deregulation of capital controls, deep and rapid privat- isation of state-owned enterprises and, perhaps the strongest unifying factor in this group – rapid and major opening up of an economy to trade and foreign direct investment'. But on each of these issues, says Kanbur, there are others (referred to as Group B types) who 'tend to lean the other way'.[6]

Ravi Kanbur not only recognizes these widely different accounts of poverty and how to reduce or eliminate it, but goes on to ask why these deep disagreements arise. We don't have to look far for some of the answers. One is, and I speak now for myself and not for him, that we come at these things from very different perspectives. Ravi Kanbur profiles Group A types as 'Finance Ministry' and Group B types as 'Civil Society'. We could equally talk about the different perspectives of officialdom and the grassroots; of the expert and the people; of rich and poor; of men and women; of still to some extent North and South; of hands-on

[5] Ravi Kanbur, 'Economic Policy, Distribution and Poverty: The Nature of Disagreements', (unpublished paper based on a presentation to the Swedish Parliamentary Commission on Global Development, 22 September 2000).

[6] Kanbur, 'Economic Policy, Distribution and Poverty', pp. 4–5.

workers and theoretical economists. As different people, in different circumstances, with different vantage points, they will have different accounts of reality. A second obvious source of disagreement is that none of us is fully informed. In a big and complex world we cannot know everything. We see a part but not the whole. As a result we may not only see the same things differently from our different perspectives, but not even be talking about the same things because of our lack of information. Ravi Kanbur gives examples of talking at cross purposes in this way. For example, overall statistics for a country may reveal an average increase in income per head of population (as they did in Ghana) while public services have declined, making education and healthcare less accessible and the buses more expensive. One vantage point and set of data lead to a statistician's view of 'reality' while another vantage point and another set of very hard facts, namely that of a woman on below-average income, unable to send her children to school or go to market on the bus, leads to quite another. To take a further example, views about future prospects for the poor may vary according to whether as a poor person you take a short-term view, or as a trade economist you take a medium-term view, or as an environmentalist you take a long-term view, and in each case you will produce data to support it. To be told that opening up markets and joining the free flow of trade will be good for the poor and that they will reap the benefits in 5 to 10 years' time is one account of your prospects. That your basic needs cannot be met today or tomorrow or for the next 5 to 10 years and that the sharp winds of open competition may indeed make things worse for a while is another account. (By then we may all be dead.) That even if trading does create wealth the mechanisms of the so-called natural world will be near to collapse in 25 years' time if we go on treating it as we do now, is another account of your prospects.

A third cause of these highly divergent views of reality to which Ravi Kanbur draws our attention is the different assumptions on which people operate. After a time these assumptions are no longer the distilled outcomes of paying careful attention to the empirical evidence but the underlying view of reality into which empirical evidence or 'the facts of the matter' now tend to fall into place. A fundamental faith in the neo-liberal economy and what it can achieve, and a fundamental distrust of it, are clearly examples – as Ravi Kanbur points out in his discussion of Market Structures and Power. Opening up trade to free competition and increasing the mobility of capital spells positive gain and increasing wealth for the first mind-set, and spells progressive disaster for smaller countries, business enterprises and unskilled labour for the other mind-set.

Seeking common ground

The 'reality' then is deep and persistent disagreements about reality (!), including the prospects for the poorest and what is to be done to ensure that the future for them is brighter than the present. To be fair, there is growing agreement in some areas between some parties. The growing consensus that both state and market have a role to play (rather than state-centred controlled economies with no free market, or free markets with little or no social controls and a minimalist state) is one of them. On the other hand, events surrounding Seattle and Genoa leading to G8 leaders taking to their bunkers to avoid conflict, are signs of a growing antagonism. Total unanimity is, of course, to be feared as much as a breakdown of co-operation. Disagreement is a necessary fact of life among mortals and a proper stimulus to critical and creative thinking. Nevertheless, we can hardly be content to leave the matter where it is. We need to find common ground for at least two reasons. First, because it is more likely (though it is not inevitable) to represent a more satisfactory account of what we are up against, and we shall only be constructive in dealing with poverty if we deal with things as they are rather than as we would like them to be or deceive ourselves into thinking them to be. Second, it seems common sense to suggest that we shall achieve more if 'Finance Ministry' and 'Civil Society', World Bank economists and people's movements, economic experts and NGOs, pull together rather than in opposite directions.

What then is to be done?

The principle, I believe, is one of thoroughgoing or radical participation. One long-standing approach to Christian social ethics has been to acknowledge the insights which faith can bring to social questions but to insist that they must co-operate hand-in-glove with other disciplines including, in the case of poverty reduction, most obviously those of the economist and the developmentalist. Not so long ago this approach was criticized for being elitist, harking back to rule by 'philosopher-kings'. The so-called experts or specialists, it was argued, whether theologians or economists, did not necessarily always know best. The real source of wisdom was the people, in this case the poor and their organizations. Popular opinion was a safer bet than that of ivory-towered academics. Both approaches of course were wrong. Both groups have important contributions to make, but neither has all the wisdom or has nothing to learn from the other. Anybody who has been involved in development knows well the danger of outside specialists assuming they know more than local poor communities on the ground, whether it is farming we are talking about or healthcare or mobilizing communities. And both the experts and the people can be held up as good illustrations of the three reasons we have cited as to why people disagree: they come at it from their own particular vantage point; they have useful but limited information; and they often fall into a mind-set of assumptions which then colour the evidence. The same goes for all the many players in poverty eradication, from the poor to the rich, the amateur to the specialist, the expatriate to the local, the government minister to the community leader, the NGO worker to the IMF official, the executive of a multinational to the worker in an income-generating project, the economist to the nomad. Between them 'reality' can fall apart.

The way forward is not to imagine that there is some correct view of things which all reasonable people will eventually recognize if only they can be helped to see it. Therein lies the tyranny of modernism and an over-confidence in universal reasons; which is never to deny that a patient sifting of evidence and paying careful attention to what lies in front of us can never clear away some errors and misunderstandings. The way out or forward is to maximize encounters (some like to talk about 'deep dialogue') between different people and groups, all of them partial in their views, all of them limited in their knowledge, all of them prone to questionable assumptions, in the hope that their partialities and limitations, which fortunately are not the same in each case, can challenge, critique, correct and complement each other and that together they may arrive at some common view –

not about everything, not for ever and probably not by the same route or for the same reasons – which is more enlightened and provides a basis for co-operation.

In the wake of the criticisms of structural adjustment policies (SAPs) and discussions and debates about cancelling the debts of the poorest countries, one focus of attention is now the Poverty Reduction Strategy Papers (PRSPs) whereby each country sets out how it will organize its internal affairs, structure its economy and plan its spending so that the resources made available through loans and debt remittance can benefit the poorest. The encouraging feature of the process by which these Papers are drawn up is that at least three main parties have to be involved: the government of the country; the external funders like the World Bank; and civil society – which means the representatives of local NGOs and people's organizations, including religious organizations, reaching right down to the grassroots. This, potentially, is a very different scenario from the World Bank imposing policies on the grounds that it knows best, or private and secret deals between the Bank and the government of the day; and is a useful step towards the radical participation which an intrinsically pluralist world requires to tackle its problems.

This kind of participation in getting a grip on a shared reality and deciding how best to respond is much more easily said than done. Levels of influence round the table, for example, will vary greatly. The confidence of some participants will be minimal. Being patient and listening will not be easy. We must leave these important questions aside in this chapter except to say that learning how to manage this radical participation and make it productive is one of the less glamorous but more significant steps on the road to poverty eradication.

Vested interests

To return to the deep disagreements over world poverty and the global economy, and the reality of divergent realities, there is at least one more reason for them which we have so far failed to mention. Many of the NGOs in the UK and elsewhere are revitalizing their campaigns for fair trade. Again there are divergent views as to whether the trading practices of the global economy are potentially good for the poor or will simply and forever do them harm. The 'Finance Ministry' of Ravi Kanbur's typology believes that poor countries can trade their way out of poverty. 'Civil Society' believes the rules favour the rich and the big multinationals and harm the poor. And to go back to the study in 24 countries, small vulnerable economies like the Windward Isles complain that what is supposed to be sauce for the poor goose, like lowering their barriers and opening up to competition, is evidently not sauce for the rich gander of the European Union. These differences arise for all the reasons already mentioned but equally or even more so because of the vested interest of the parties involved.

One further point is worth noting with reference to trade. The Overseas Development Institute (ODI) of London, among other research bodies, tries to take a fairly detached view of these things (even though detached views don't exist) and having no particular axe to grind (so to speak) offers a less partial view of reality. One result is some useful briefing papers on poverty-related issues, which can inform the thinking of policy-makers and campaigners (an important element in the 'radical participation' we have been talking about). Sheila Page, for example, of the ODI has written extensively and helpfully about trade, an extremely complicated subject indeed. She makes the interesting point that whatever the merits of the arguments about protecting markets or opening them up, about tariffs and subsidies, about privileged quotas and all the rest, all these external conditions of global trading can be far less significant in dealing with poverty than internal conditions of governance within a country.[7] To put it another way, even relatively favourable external conditions will easily count for little or nothing as far as the poor are concerned if governments are weak, inept, corrupt or acting in ways that are self-seeking and protect the interests of the few rather than in ways which benefit the whole of society and, above all, the poorest.

Both these observations – one about vested interests and the other about the crucial role of governments – bring us to the central issue of power. There are three points to be clear about. First, our vested interest will colour the way we see the world and the 'reality' we believe we have to deal with. Who are the terrorists and who are the freedom fighters is not entirely decided but is considerably affected by where your interests lie; so is the

[7] At her lecture in the Faculty of Law, University of Barcelona, 4 October 2001.

soundness of the laws and the economic regime you live under or refuse to accept; so is the adequacy of policies to do with the euro; so is your perception of the moral character of the poor, the immigrant and the unemployed. Second, human beings tend to behave in ways that advance what they perceive to be their real interest to the detriment of the interests of others. Reinhold Niebuhr famously observed that we are even more likely to behave like this as social groups, classes and nations than as individuals. [8] I do not believe we do so because we are simply perverse but because we are insecure both in a practical sense (the immigrant is a threat to my job) and a related existential sense (in the end life presents us with more not-knowing than knowing). As a result we are self-protective. We shield ourselves as best we can and hence become egocentric and destructive of the lives and prospects of others. This is the factor which in the end decides which side you are on in any war, whether it is against terrorism or against poverty or against unfair trade or against capitalism or against so-called illegal immigration. The third point to be clear about is certainly not that the powerful or the rich are morally inferior to the weak or the poor, rather, the powerful or rich have far greater opportunities to behave egotistically and therefore destructively. They have the means to protect and promote their own self-interests whereas the weak and the poor do not. The 'reality' is of a highly unequal struggle and it is not surprising that it sits cheek by jowl with a highly unequal world.

Issues of power

If the reality we face is, among other things, a significant imbalance of power, what then is to be done to eradicate poverty? First, what is never sufficient is to leave the poor to the mercy, or generosity, of the charity of the rich, because the rich will go so far with their aid and their giving but no further. Charity, as we know, on however grand a scale, is not a way of changing things but of keeping things as they are, and all the more effectively because of its apparent benevolence.

---

[8] See, for example, his *Moral Man and Immoral Society* (New York: Charles Scribner's Sons, 1932).

Second, realism about power should not lead to cynicism about the kind of radical participation we have been considering, where partial views and incomplete understandings have an opportunity to inform, critique and complement each other. It should, however, make us acutely aware that such exercises in participation are as infected with issues of power as is everything else. Information can be withheld, for example; and the World Bank and IMF can pull the plug on debt cancellation in a way that governments and civil society cannot.

Third, imbalances of power are not put right by reversals of power so that the mighty are toppled from their thrones and the poor get their chance to rule the world. Perhaps the poor should be given the chance but, once rich and powerful, they will behave like their predecessors. The strategy is not to reverse power but to balance power or, more helpfully, to disperse power between counterbalancing and countervailing centres of power, so that no one has too much and can lord it over the rest without restraint. That is one of the underlying principles of democracy. It is why we need not only instruments of world governance like the United Nations and the World Trade Organization to regulate trade and the market place, but why we have to make them more democratic than they are now. Yet a concern to make sure that power does not have free reign but is checked by others leads in other directions as well. It increases our enthusiasms for a strengthened civil society and it increases our anxieties about the apparent weakening of the nation state in the global economy compared to the power of capital and the multinationals.

Fourth, if we are going to be serious about a world where power is dispersed a good deal more than it is at present (where even those who are prepared to sacrifice their own lives in suicidal attempts to change things don't apparently have all that much success, faced with the powers that be) it is not enough to give the relatively powerless more opportunities to share in decision-making. We have to build up their capacity to make the most of those opportunities and to be genuinely influential. One example is the WTO, frequently accused of being the playground of the rich trading nations who, under pressure from the multinationals, make the laws to suit themselves. It is not enough to insist that the poorest countries have a seat at the table, as they do. It is not just a matter of presence but of influence. A major trading nation can afford to send a whole delegation of officials and experts to WTO meetings so that its representatives at the table are well briefed and can make their voices heard in a whole range of meetings, often going on at the same time. A poorer country can hardly afford to send a single representative let alone the civil servants required as back-up and to brief on highly technical and complex negotiations. Another example is the round table, advocated for poor countries as a mechanism by which to manage debt relief and draw up country strategies for poverty reduction. Civil society organizations would be members of those round tables, but again it is one thing to be there and another to have the capacity to be influential. If they represent a large constituency they may have some political weight, but they need to be able to make their case with knowledge and confidence – and when it comes to religious communities, not just Christian but of all faiths, what does 'confidence' mean for them? Of course they must recognize that poverty reduction has to do with technical and economic issues about which they should not be entirely unsophisticated; but poverty reduction also has to do with moral and spiritual issues. Here they should learn to play to their strengths and not always be drawn onto other people's ground where they are less articulate, but draw the other parties onto theirs.

Fifth, one blaring weakness in any strategy that aims at counterbalancing power is that the initiative once again seems to lie with the powerful, who are unlikely to seize it to any significant extent. As a contribution to eradicating poverty they are invited to share power, or cede power; but it is not in the nature of egocentric social groups with vested interest to do so. So, a number of other complementary strategies and considerations become equally important. Let me mention four. None is foolproof or self-sufficient. One is paying attention to international law and systems of justice including international law-keeping as much as peace-keeping and international courts of justice, a theme taken up by Rowan Williams in his reflections following September 11th and his plea to stop the talk of 'war' and to start talking more about the due processes of international law. Most of the powers that be are unlikely to volunteer to behave very well in the interests of the poorest. We must strengthen international law and our capacity to enforce it to make sure that we do good – or at least less harm – even if we do not wish to. A human rights approach to development fits well with this kind of thinking. We are not talking about what it may be desirable to achieve in terms of education and healthcare and secure livelihoods if and when the resources we can spare for aid and development make it possible. We are talking about what all human beings are entitled to here and now and what it is therefore the legal duty of governments to deliver according to international law rooted in human rights. The Christian community, incidentally, may at this point be far more Christian if it spoke about the law rather more than about the Gospel. In doing so it might contribute more effectively to our neighbours' good – and it is in contributing to their good that we show towards them what we call Christian love.

Another strategy which becomes important, given the fact that the powerful are unlikely to share much of their power, is promoting a more compelling vision of what is sometimes referred to as 'the common good' or what might better be called 'the common self-interest'. Insecure people and groups and nations and coalitions act in their own self-interest and against the interest of others. Taking a longer and more inclusive view, their perceived self-interest may not be in their interest at all. Recent events suggest that may well be true of a world deeply divided between rich and poor. In the end it may not only oppress the poor but endanger the rich as it erupts in violent frustration and rage. The debate about the environment raises similar issues. But if a just world and an environmentally sustainable world is a better world for everyone it is not a vision we articulate very clearly with the kind of 'empirical' detail that makes it interesting, and it is not a 'gospel' we preach with much charisma or success. Here is an urgent, constructive task, needing to be done in a highly participative way, crucial to the future of the poor, that ought to attract those who believe they are creative just as much as insecure and egotistical human beings.

Two other initiatives both have to be taken up mainly by the powerless. First, they have to increase their own power, rather than wait to be given power, by building up their own networks of solidarity. This was another strong conclusion that emerged from the recent study in 24 countries. Issues of management, so that networks and alliances become effective political instruments and not just talking shops, for example, are as significant here as they are in efforts to maximize radical participation.

Second, the poor and the weak need 'strategies of resistance' which will never entirely counteract the influence of the powers that be but make it a little less easy for those powers to overwhelm them. In the old language of development, it may decrease the levels of dependency. One example is the discussion about 'internalized economies'. No region or community or country can cut itself off from the outside world, in this case the global economy, and be entirely independent of its influence which may, if defied, turn punitive. But by developing ways of maximizing the use of its own internal resources and skills and fostering a socially moderated internal market it may be able to lessen the degree to which it must always bow to the dictates of the external world. Increasing the power of the weak in ways that do not necessarily require the strong to make the first move and cede their power (though eventually they may be forced to do so) used to be thought of merely in military terms: like 'arming guerrillas', as Christian Aid, rather romantically, used to be accused of doing! Today we have to think much more in organizational and economic terms, but the underlying principle is the same.

Informative and supportive faith

So far we have talked about the divergence of views on world poverty and what is to be done about it, including the confidence we have in the global economic system to put an end to it. We have looked at why these differences and disagreements arise and what is to be done about them. I personally stand with those who, though critical of the global economy, set out to reform it and regulate it better to work for the poor. I do not set out to replace it, partly no doubt because I benefit from it and partly because I haven't the wit to see a radical alternative. Within that reformist context I have highlighted two areas of central importance. One is maximizing radical participation in policy- and decision-making. The other is addressing the perennial issue of power. I want in conclusion to make one or two remarks of an overtly theological nature.

To go back to the overall theme and that word 'reality', Christian faith over the centuries has come to certain conclusions about 'reality'. It purports to tell us what the world is really like: not just how things 'ought' to be (the impression too many Christians preachers and teachers tend to give), but how things really 'are'. It arrives at these conclusions by way of an endless interaction between its fascination with Jesus of Nazareth and the events surrounding his birth, life and death, and its experience of life in this world: an interaction which runs both ways and where both the Jesus-events and subsequent experience affect what for the time being Christians confess to be their understanding of reality.

This Christian view of reality has of course exactly the same character as the other views of reality we have been discussing, like the 'real' prospects for the poor and whether or not the global economy is 'really' likely to do them good or harm. Without denying areas of agreement, Christian perceptions differ, and for much the same reason. Those involved in coming to theological conclusions are, on the one hand, partial in their views and limited in their knowledge; on the other hand, they too have their vested interests which they are more likely to safeguard success-fully the more powerful they are. The stark contrast between the account which Western Christianity has generally given of reality (as an aggressively missionary movement with a very private and personal spirituality) and the liberation theologies of the South (as a revolutionary movement with a highly political spirituality) – one the account of the powerful, the other an account at least adopted by the poor – is well known evidence of that. The inevitable partiality of Christian theology (or Christian accounts of reality) means that here as elsewhere we must maximize participation, ensuring that theology is a community activity where the various limitations and biases of rich and poor, specialist and lay, men and women, North and South, correct and complement each other; and once again we must pay attention to the difficult issues of power, to which voices prevail and for what good reason.

So, when we say that Christian faith has reached its own conclusions about the reality we are encouraged to face up to, we realize that things are not quite so simple as that. More likely, different forms of Christian faith have reached different conclu-sions. Nevertheless, at any one time it is possible, and presumably necessary, for any Christian or Christian community to make up their minds and confess what for them those conclusions are and to proceed from there. How then will they impinge on our concerns about the future of the poor? The answer is probably: 'in many and various ways'; but I shall mention only two. One I shall call 'informative' and the other 'supportive'.

1. First, Christian conclusions about reality will inform our views about the prospects for the poor and what can best be done to eradicate poverty. These conclusions are not sufficient on their own and we shall be of little use to the poor or anyone else if we do not take other disciplines, both theoretical and practical, carefully into account. But they do, nevertheless, inform what we do, and in my experience rather more directly and straightforwardly than some of the discussions about, say, middle axioms and intermediary principles, might suggest.

It is obvious from what I have said above that one of the most relevant and useable Christian insights in my experience of working on world poverty issues has to do with the human insecurity which leads to the egocentric defensive behaviour which safeguards our own interests and is so disregarding and destructive of the interests of others, and which we will practise whenever we have the power to do so. This is the reality we have to face up to and we shall do no one much good if we ignore it. We build it as an assumption into all our policies and we test all our policies against it. Its usability and relevance is not only reflected in the emphasis to be placed on governance and international law; it runs right down to the micro-levels of development policy and practice. I remember, for example, the trust placed in local village communities in Bangladesh to operate programmes for the benefit of the community: fish farms and banana plantations; only to find that the slightly less poor in the village – and therefore slightly more powerful – were manipulating the whole system to benefit themselves. It is not only the G8 and our rich selves that need watching, but also the relatively poor.

There are, of course, many other such Christian insights into reality. The inevitable limitations of all human beings is one, as is our interdependence with the so-called natural world. Other Christian views on what human beings are really like as individuals and social creatures lead us to support human rights but also to question them. The point is that 'Christian Realism', if you like to call it that, or the Christian understanding of what reality is like, plays an informative role and helps to shape policy and practice.

But a phrase like 'Christian Realism' is almost always heard as striking a sombre note. Things are neither as easy, nor hopeful, nor upbeat as we might like to think. The same is true of the phrase: 'facing up to reality'. Only when things are rather difficult and unwelcome do we talk about 'facing up' to them at all. We can certainly do without those Christians who indulge in wishful thinking or sentimental responses to highly complex and intractable problems – like world poverty. 'Get real' we quite rightly say. But we should not neglect what might be called the more positive side of Christian Realism and we must allow that, too, to inform our policies and practice. Human nature, for example, is characterized by at least two intrinsic qualities, not one. It is self-regarding and therefore destructive (what Christians refer to, not always helpfully, as 'sinful'). But it is also generous, selfless and creative (what Christians refer to as 'the image of God'). Both are part of reality: the reality we need to deal with if we are to be of use and not make inappropriate and unhelpful moves. Again, Christianity has much to say about the dynamics which disrupt our human relations and make people poor in body, mind and spirit. But it also has much to say about the dynamics which are productive of better human relations and make people happier, enriched and fulfilled. Christianity speaks about the realities which break us but also the realities which make us. These creative dynamics have to do with solidarity and inclusion, with participation, generosity and persistence, all of which have deep roots in the gospels and Christian doctrine; and, while it will be a useless strategy to combat poverty with appeals to our better nature and sense of human obligation without allowing for the fact that we are prone to do each other down, it will be an equally useless strategy to combat poverty which carefully puts in place all the safeguards against the misuse of power but never allows for the generosity of spirit that, according to the story of Jesus, can make all things new. An over-obsession with facing up to grim reality may leave creative reality with too little room to breathe. I think it is an area which Christian social ethics, and certainly my own, tends to neglect.

In recognizing this informative role of Christianity, shaping policy and practice in the struggle against poverty, I do not wish to overestimate the uniqueness of its contribution nor underplay the contribution of, say, other religious traditions. Indeed, I think Western Christianity in particular has grown rather tired and difficult to disentangle from the political and economic 'realities' which members of other religious traditions blame for keeping them poor. I also think that other religions might have some refreshing things to say to us about more holistic approaches to development.[9]

2. I mentioned two ways in which Christian conclusions about reality impinge on our concerns about eradicating poverty. The first I called 'informative' and the second 'supportive'. Faith can play a supportive role by undergirding and surrounding our endeavours with the encouragement, inspiration, motivation and justification they need and by putting them in a setting or within a story about our lives where they add up and make sense.

Supportive stories easily run into two kinds of danger. They can support people in wrong endeavours. Theology has always been good at that, and history is full of examples – from the Crusades to foreign missions to apartheid. But even if the endeavours seem to be in tune with Jesus of Nazareth and are intent on bringing good news to the poor, they can be told by ignoring the facts rather than facing up to reality. Theology has been good at those stories as well: that the sufferings of the poor can somehow be explained satisfactorily; that the Gospel of Christ has the power to redeem the world as it spreads across the continents and islands; that steady progress will be made towards a utopian kingdom of God; that the back is broken of the evil powers and that they are all but overcome; that the poor will inherit the earth. All of them, if true, would be encouraging, inspiring, highly motivating stories to rehearse repeatedly in our liturgy, putting our lives together again and making sense of it all. But they are not true.

Our faith can play a highly supportive role if it can tell a story in the full blaze of reality, a reality which reveals a great deal of compassion and creativity and courage but also reveals a world in which we have good reason to feel pessimistic about the future for the poor whose numbers increase, whose misery does not go away, whose distance from the affluent elite gets wider, and who get the attentions of the powerful not when it suits the common good but when it suits the interests of the rich (as, for example, in the case of debt relief or Palestine).

The supportive Christian story I sometimes tell myself for real is not about progressive transformation brought about by the Gospel; though I do not rule out the possibility of change for the better in any set of circumstances, however desperate. And the story I tell myself is not about an underlying reality which,

---

[9] See Chapter 8 below.

however obscure, will ensure that all will be well at the end of the long day, though I do not entirely rule out the possibility of belonging to a benign universe. The story I sometimes tell myself is about a God who, confronted with an extremely unpromising scenario like the primeval chaos of the deep and the even deeper chaos of our unloving, destructive insecurities chose, not once at the moment of so-called creation but, according to the clue given to us in Christ, chose all the time, forever incarnate in our world, to hope in us or believe in us, that this unpromising material had potential, and in so doing created that potential; just as when we choose to believe in others as well as ourselves, we create potential in them, whether they are like us or unlike us, weak or powerless, rich or poor. The story I sometimes tell myself is of a Christlike God, not deciding that reality looks promising enough to have hope, but choosing to have hope and in so doing filling life with promise. The poorest of the poor, crucified in a political intifada, has no reason to hope, but chooses to do so and thereby adds to reality that belief in it and its potential which is at the heart of creativity.

That is the story which supports my own endeavours, such as they are, and I suspect that, tentative as it is in the telling, it is just as important for me as all the important insights I think I can cull from my faith to inform my social practice. It is certainly the Eucharistic food and drink on which they are nourished.

4

Poverty and Globalization[1]

I want to develop two lines of thought – one about the nature of
the disagreement over the global economy and its impact on
poverty, and a second about the causes of this disagreement.

The nature of the disagreement

The global economy is not the whole of globalization but it is a
very large part of it and it is the part we shall be campaigning
about on May Day. It is 'global' – or universal – in at least three
ways. First, because to many it seems to be the only economic
system left after the collapse of socialism and the state-centred
economies of the East. It is the universal answer. 'There is no
alternative.' We have reached 'the end of history' because in
economic terms there is nowhere left to go. Second, it is global
because the transactions of the global economy cover huge
distances. Goods and services are bought and sold between one
continent and another. India handles the computers for the
London underground railway system. The supermarket shelves
are stacked with products from all over the world. Third, it is
global because it is all-embracing. It touches East and West, North
and South. It affects us all, though not in the same way, for good
or ill.

What are some of its other features? First, it prefers our
economic affairs to be run by private enterprise rather than by

---

[1] One of a series of lectures given in Wesley's Chapel in the City of London in
April 2002.

64

governments and public bodies. Things are done more efficiently that way. Which is why, for example, countries that want loans are encouraged to privatize public services, like the water supply. And it is why transnational corporations have become much bigger players in the global economy than many a nation state, with much more power to get their way. Second, and it is close to the first, the global economy, sometimes called a free market economy, prefers to let the market find its own level. If there is a demand for coffee, people will pay for it. If there's too much of it about, the price will fall, and if there is too little then the price will rise. That's how it should be. Supply and demand is the best mechanism for sorting things out. Open competition is the order of the day. Start interfering and subsidizing and the market will be distorted. Not everyone plays by the rules but at least we know what the rules are. Third, the global economy wants open frontiers and no barriers. We call it 'free trade'. Nothing should get in the way of the free flow of buying and selling between nations and continents. Trade barriers, protectionism, import duties and tariffs should as far as possible be swept away. Finally, the global economy seems greatly preoccupied with trading money. There are statistics for this and I am not going into statistics here, but if you roll the reel back, say 100 years, there was already a global economy, with buying and selling between one part of the world and another, but what was being bought and sold in those days was largely raw materials, like cotton, and manufactured goods. Today they represent only a small percentage of the transactions of the global economy. Mostly it is money which is bought and sold, between Tokyo and the City of London and Wall Street and the rest, in order to make more goods and services but also, and often, simply to make more money.

Much of this globalization, as we all know, has been aided and abetted by the advance of information technology, whereby orders can be given, deals can be made, money can be switched and frontiers can be crossed and recrossed in the twinkling of an eye or the twitch of a mouse.

Here then is the global economy: all-embracing, characterized by privatization, free markets, open borders and a striking preoccupation with making money.

And, as most of us know, there are two diametrically opposed opinions about it. On the one hand are those who believe it is the best hope of the poor. Most of the economists in the World Bank and the IMF share that opinion. It offers hope above all because it creates more wealth. Less is said about distributing wealth, but a great deal is said about wealth creation, in the firm belief that even if the rich do get even richer, everyone will benefit and all the boats will rise. Poverty is dealt with fundamentally by economic growth, and this global economic order is the way to achieve it.

Two implications follow. One is that it is the best hope for the poor if the poor, especially poor countries and governments, will bring their own failing economies into line with its rules. When the World Bank and the IMF had a great deal to say about 'structural adjustment policies' (SAPs) and required countries to adopt them, that was the turnaround they were trying to bring about. The other implication is that the global economy is the best hope for the poor if the poor will only join it along with the rest of us, swim with the tide of history, stop trying to barricade themselves in, and seize the chance to trade across frontiers and grow prosperous. Where they have been brave enough to try, it is argued, it has worked. They have met with success. They have traded their way out of poverty.

Yet if some believe the global economy is the best hope of the poor, others believe it does the poor no good at all. Of course, there are other objections to 'globalization'. Some of the relatively rich don't like it because it's a threat to the environment and gobbles up limited natural resources. Others see it as a threat to cultural diversity as McDonald's and Pepsi rule the world. Whatever the truth in all of that, the main objection is that the global economy does not enrich the poor but impoverishes them. It aggravates their poverty. At best it maintains and perpetuates it rather than redeems it.

The evidence quoted is familiar enough. The gap between rich and poor grows wider and wider, between countries and within countries, and that includes our country. Whatever the merits of structural adjustment policies may be, and no one can quarrel with trying to get an economy on its feet, the poor seem to suffer the worst effects as jobs are cut back, prices rise and schools and hospitals become more expensive. A friend from Zambia wept in my office because of what he believed were the consequences of structural adjustment policies and privatization on his people. Again, debt is an intrinsic feature of the world economy. Money has to be lent and borrowed if money is to be made. But if the system works well enough for rich countries that can manage their debts, and even works for the elite of some poor countries, it has plunged the poorest who borrowed none of the money and enjoyed none of its benefits into deeper misery as debt repayments take precedence over food and education and healthcare. And while the global economy touches almost everyone, its benefits pass all too many people by. It is marked by exclusion: exclusion from its benefits, exclusion from its opportunities, exclusion from its investments, exclusion from its control and, maybe worst of all, exclusion of the millions that it doesn't any longer need for its success.

Two important points need to be made about this fundamental divergence of views.

First, there is no necessary disagreement between the two camps about the unacceptability of poverty, or gross inequality, or marginalization. You can believe in the global economy, as many of the people I know and work with passionately do; and you can dismiss the global economy along with the anti-globalization campaigners; but you can still join hands and cry together against injustice. You can disagree about the cause and you can disagree about the cure but you can still agree about injustice; you can still agree that it exists and is contrary to everything we have learned as Christian people from the Old Testament prophets and Jesus himself and the great crowd of witnesses who have sought after God's kingdom and his righteousness; and you can still be committed as a Christian and a human being to getting rid of it. For or against the economic system, people on both sides can be and are against injustice.

Let me remind you of two of the most obvious examples of that injustice in the world today. One is about work and the other is about visas. When it comes to work, rich and poor can both be work-shy and lazy, and prefer to sit in the sun or take whatever handouts they can get. But most people, rich or poor alike, are hard-working. They have a sense of pride and a desire to make their own way and earn their keep and look after themselves and their families. But hard work doesn't bring comparable, let alone equal, rewards. The rich can work hard; the poor often work harder, and a poor woman works even harder than poor men: fetching and carrying water, cooking and washing, carrying and caring for children, cleaning the house, looking after domestic animals, going to the fields – and all for little or nothing. Equally hard work over long hours does not reap equitable returns.

Then there are the visas. If a wealthy financier wishes to move his money from one country or continent to another, not to invest in its future and take the rough with the smooth along with its people, but to speculate and make more money – and I have literally seen it happen in Macedonia and in the UK (in Longbridge, Birmingham) – he needs no visa to allow his money to travel. He needs no passport for his money to cross the borders. He needs no entry permit. His money can move at will, often at the flick of a switch, to make more money, or avoid the taxes on the money he has already. But what about a poor man or woman with only the work of their hands and their skills to travel with, who wish to go from one country to another to try and make a better living and take care of their families? For them the border-crossing by boat, by train, by night, by lorry, by whatever, is far more difficult, even impossible, with visas and passports and permits and identity cards all required as well as excuses, if they are not to be turned back as bogus asylum seekers or illegal immigrants. Money can travel and prosper. The poor man cannot.

The second important point is that there is no necessary difference in the morality of those who believe the global economy is good for the poor and those who believe it does them no good at all. If we join the anti-globalization campaigners we cannot necessarily claim the moral high ground; and it would be dishonest and unfair to suggest that members of the World Bank staff, for example, are indifferent to the poor and less committed than those who demonstrate against their policies and practices. Both sides can have moral integrity. Both sides can abhor poverty and wish to put an end to it. Where they disagree is about how to do it.

Demonizing the opposition can miss the point and let us off the hook. The most important argument may not be a moral argument but a technical one: not about who is better but how best to get things done. So, where lies our responsibility as Christian people? If we really want to love our neighbour and actually do our neighbour a bit of good, the biggest challenge is not to have a hot head but a cool head and a clear one. We are against injustice and poverty but, if we believe the present economic system will never put matters right, it is our Christian vocation to find a better one. We must stand up and be counted, not just for what we are against but for what we are for. The biblical tradition says 'No' to injustice but it says 'Yes' to a new creation. It calls us to break down what should not stand but, even more urgently, it calls us to be creative and constructive and to build new worlds.

In general, we have been better at saying 'No' or keeping quiet than proposing alternatives, or we are sidetracked into the more comfortable territory of debate about spirituality and more holistic approaches to life and neglected cultural issues. They are all important, but they can never supplant the fundamental importance of finding a way to make the world's economy work so that everyone can have enough food and education and shelter and healthcare and a decent standard of living. Economics are not everything – of course they are not. But very little else is going to count if the basic economic necessities of life are not taken care of.

So, if we don't like this global economy, we are required as Christians to campaign for what we do like. We are not just 'breakers'. We are called to be 'makers'. That seems to me to have at least three practical implications.

First, as Christians we should recognize the importance of research into economic issues and alternatives and be ready to honour and support it. The Christian Aids and CAFODs and Tearfunds and Jubilee Campaigns of this world should not have to apologize for one minute when they build up and resource and co-ordinate think tanks and research departments with our money, and get their minds to work: on restructuring the global economy so that it favours the poor; or on trading regulations that give everyone a chance to sell and buy in the market place; or on global taxation systems that might redistribute wealth and even create it; or on internalized economies that make maximum use of a community's own resources so that they are not completely dependent on an often hostile outside world; or on better ways to handle debt and the so-called economic basket cases; or on economic systems that respect and reward everybody's contributions. As Christians we must be economically as well as theologically literate. We must campaign for what will work. We must be clever enough to confront the opposition on its own economic grounds and on its own terms. We must express our opposition to injustice and our compassion for the poor not just by shouting the negatives on the streets, and not just by giving our money to emergency appeals and development projects and programmes, but by backing with our money organizations like the New Economics Foundation in the UK,[2] the policy-makers of the development agencies, and some of the exciting research units on poverty in our universities; and we should impress on a rising generation that if they feel called by Christ to put first his kingdom, then in this day and age they should seriously consider a vocation to development economics.

The second practical implication is that we should insist that any research into alternatives to the global economy should be carried out in a thoroughly participatory way. Theoretical economists sitting in universities and banks and agencies and research units have a big part to play, but they cannot deliver by themselves. Committed and clever people from our own Northern culture, brought up in a Western rationalist tradition, have a part to play, but they cannot deliver by themselves either. The search for alternatives must involve people on the ground, especially poor people, with their untidy experience and the kind of knowledge that can only be gained from patience and practice. Like the rest of us they do not know everything but they are just as wise as we are, and we cannot be wise without them.

There is a third practical implication. The general run of us ordinary, everyday Christians are not competent to go and argue the toss with Treasury officials, or transnational corporations, or the staff of the World Bank and the IMF or the WTO. We must, nevertheless, take our cue from those who are, and back them up with our campaigning power on the streets, with our consumer power in the superstores and financial and investment institutions, with the power of our faith and of our prayers: powers which we still fail even to begin to exploit for the sake of the poor, or honour as authentic forms of Christian discipleship.

So my first line of argument is to be absolutely clear that a large part of what we are about when we face up to the so-called opposition is not a moral argument with them but a technical argument about what will work better for the poorest of the poor than the present global economic system. If we don't like what

---

[2] The New Economics Foundation, based in London, is a charity working to develop new economic ideas that put people and planet first, and to change the economic rules accordingly.

we've got we are called as Christians to positively seek out, advocate and experiment with a new economic order.

The causes of the disagreement

Turning to the second line of argument, it is important to ask why this division of opinion occurs. Why do these diametrically opposite views arise: one believing that the global economy is the only hope for the poor; the other believing it is no good for the poor at all? Of course there are lots of reasons. We come at these things from different angles. We have different histories and backgrounds and experiences. We make different assumptions which tend to colour the evidence. One person's knowledge and experience is different from another's and all of our views are partial because none of us can ever know it all.

But, over and above all this, we know very well there is one highly significant reason why we are attracted to one position rather than another. It is hugely dependent on where our self-interests lie, or where we think they lie. If we think a policy will benefit us, however little it may benefit anyone else, we tend to be in favour of it. If we think a policy will be to our disadvantage, even if it benefits other people, we are more than likely to be against it, though we usually try to find high sounding and objective reasons for doing so, rather than selfish ones.

Opinions divide according to self-interest. Here again there is no intrinsic difference between the two sides of the economic argument or between rich and poor. Those who take one view cannot claim the selfless high ground over those who take the opposite view. Self-interest is always busy at work on all sides.

Take theology, as a quite different example from the economy. It can be argued that the Western Church – our Church – has been dominated for much of its history by a theology which focuses on our sinful disobedience, our broken relationship with God, the punishment we deserve under God's law, and the forgiveness and reconciliation made possible by the sacrifice of Christ if only we will repent and put our faith and trust in him. It is a theology which tends to focus on us as individuals and our private lives and innermost relations with God. It is a very personal theology. It applies to everyone, rich and poor alike, since all are sinners. It prioritizes no one, and it is all too easy to accept its invitation and turn to Christ and find hope and comfort without any change in the social order whatsoever. It is a theology that is attractive to powerful people whose vested interest is in keeping the social order as it is because it benefits them. And the Western Church has generally been the Church of powerful people, who have tended to rule their world.

The theology that has characterized some of the churches of the South in recent years is quite different. We call it 'liberation theology'. It does not offer personal salvation through Christ without any social change but a highly political social revolution where everything changes, and freedom in Christ is not so much freedom from guilt and sin but freedom from oppression and injustice. It prioritizes the poor and says they must come first. It is a theology which is attractive to powerless people and communities whose vested interest is in getting rid of a social order which does them no favours and replacing it with one where they might have a chance to spread their wings and prosper.

One of these theologies may well be right and the other wrong. Both may contain a measure of the truth. That is not the point. The point is that what divides us in favour of one or the other is where our self-interest lies: for the rich it lies in the status quo; for the poor, in radical change.

The same is true when we opt not for a theology but for an economic system. There is an important technical argument to be had about what will work; and there is a highly significant vested-interest argument to be had about what works for me and for us – whether we can prosper in the economic order as it is or whether we only see ourselves going to the wall unless it is radically changed.

All of us, rich and poor, relatively rich and relatively poor, have our own self-interests and tend to act on them. That is not the difference between us. The real difference is that we don't all have the same opportunity to act on them. Some are in a far stronger position to pursue their self-interests than others: the USA is in a stronger position that Iraq; Israel is in a stronger position than the Palestinians; transnational corporations are in a stronger position than coffee growers in Ethiopia; the G8 is in a stronger position than highly indebted poor countries (HIPCs); the World Bank and the IMF are in a stronger position than many a poor nation state; the middle classes are in a stronger position than those who stand in the benefits queue; citizens of democracies like ours are in a stronger position than people in countries where civil society can hardly afford to organize at all; and citizens of industrial countries are in a stronger position than immigrants from poor ones. The crucial issue when push comes to shove is the issue of power.

So, besides campaigning for an improved economic order we should also be in the corridors of power and out on the streets campaigning and arguing on at least two further fronts.

First, if it's fundamentally a matter of power, we don't want to campaign for a reversal of power: a kind of Magnificat upside-down world where the mighty are removed from their thrones and the poor get their chance to sit on them for a change. It might be only fair to give the poor a turn but it won't make any difference in the long run because, once there, they'll start behaving like their predecessors. No, the campaigning strategy is not to reverse power but to share the power: 'just share' power if you like, so that everyone has a better chance of pursuing their own self-interest and no one is left with so much power to push everyone else around that their self-interest dominates.

This is a strategy which digs deep into our Christian under-standing of human nature. On the one hand, we all reflect the image of God. We are all capable of being generous and creative – and of imaginatively making the new economic worlds we talked about in our first line of argument. On the other hand, our nature is profoundly insecure. We always tend to protect ourselves and our self-interest and use whatever power we have to do so. So, according to Christian Realism, power has to be shared: your power has to check mine and mine has to check yours and someone else has to check us both if we are to prevent the worst of injustice, including economic injustice.

That is why, for example, we raise the alarm if Malawi has a weak voice at the World Trade Organization while the USA or the UK has a loud one which can drown out all the rest. That is why we raise the alarm if transnational corporations and their money are able to travel the world unfettered while nation states struggle to control their own financial affairs and care for their people. That is why we raise the alarm if democracy is so weak and unreal that corrupt dictators can have their way and steal or misuse the limited resources of their country. That is why we raise the alarm if deals are done about loans for development and debt repayment and poverty reduction plans without local people, and if their organized networks (which we call 'civil society') don't have a seat at the table and a say in what is going on. That is why we raise the alarm when poor people and badly paid workers and people on even less than a minimum wage are marginalized and divided and organizationally weakened so that those who exploit them can trample on their rights and dignities as human beings.

Opinions divide because of where our self-interests lie. None of us is free from that. The difference is that some of us have more opportunity to pursue and protect those interests than others. We have more power. So if we want 'just shares' we must test every proposal for economic reform to see whether it will concentrate power even more in a few hands or begin to share it out, or at least restrain it by international law based on human rights. And if we want to show our Christian love for our neighbours, of course we should be sympathetic and generous and kind-hearted, but we shall do our neighbours little good if we back off from the issue of power.

But recognizing the significant role played by self-interest leads to a second campaigning strategy. Madeline Bunting, the journalist, once said in an article in the *Guardian* newspaper that: 'guilt is a crucial part of the Western moral tradition ... guilt is what is most likely to prompt you to change'.[3] I don't think I altogether agree with her. Guilt is certainly a crucial part of the Western moral tradition. I have just indicated that in my rather crude account of the general tone of Western theology. But it seems to me we handle our guilt rather well so that we learn to live with it in a state of forgiving acceptance and it changes nothing. I doubt that 'guilt' is most likely to prompt us to change. It could be 'fear' that will change us. Above all, it will be a shift in our perceptions of where our real self-interest lies which is most likely to prompt us to change.

The US oil industry, for example, will go on fighting to protect its supplies across the world or securing its supplies within its own safer Northern American borders, independent of the hazards and misfortunes of the rest of the world; it will go on allowing the car industry and its opportunities for jobs and profits to grow, until or unless the growing environmental catastrophe caused by conflict, and the destruction of the land, and the pollution of the

---

[3] *Guardian*, 11 February 2002.

air, choking and flooding human life into abject misery through storm and tempest and the rising of the waters, is brought home to us, creating a quite proper and well-founded fear, and altering our perceptions of where our real self-interest lies.

The rich, including ourselves, will go on making money as fast as we can, apparently at the expense of the majority rather than for everybody's benefit, until and unless the explosive potential of the situation we are creating is brought home to us, with its deep divides and growing resentments, and we are instilled with a quite proper and well-founded fear of a global conflict that will not just terrify, but consume us all; and our perceptions as to where our real self-interests lie are radically changed.

For as long as we believe it is in our self-interest to go on as we are: making money, maintaining poverty, widening the gap between rich and poor, marginalizing millions by missing them out or not missing them at all, putting the earth which sustains us at risk, then we shall go on as we are. So, our strategy must be first to frighten people to death with the consequences of what they are doing and then, second, to persuade them that their self-interest lies elsewhere than they think, in a more attractive alternative to a global rat-race, which takes a more rounded and co-operative and tolerant approach to human life on earth in which no one is the loser, not even ourselves, and all shall have prizes because all have won their share in the common good. The fundamental task is a massive shift in perceptions and values comparable to Margaret Thatcher's achievement a generation ago, when she persuaded people in the UK to be selfish and forget about society.

In the Christian tradition from which I come, many a preacher of a past generation used that first campaigning tactic to win converts, and often to good effect. He (and it was always 'he') would make it absolutely clear in a forcible way that his congregation were sinners, up to no good, doing what was evil in God's sight, condemned as guilty and heading for the rich punishment they deserved, and it was all on a rather personal and individual and private level. We are called to make it absolutely clear to even bigger 'secular' congregations that we are up to no good and largely responsible for it and heading for the dire consequences of what we are doing: a wasteland instead of a homeland, but all on a much more social and community and public level.

The old-fashioned preacher, however, was never really out to frighten people to death but to frighten them into life – and we must do the same. The old-fashioned preacher knew there was more to it than bad news. He had good news to preach as well. In our day that cannot mean frantically preaching a Gospel calculated to benefit the Church and recruit new members into its ranks. It certainly cannot be the prosperity Gospel which gains ground among both rich and poor. It has to be the good news that there is a common good or a common self-interest that can include us all and that, while we can never realize it completely, as if the kingdom of God could come on earth, we can set our eyes on it and move nearer to it with every step we take, rather than move further away.

We are partly back to our calling to say what we are 'for', not just what we are against, and to make sure we are well informed when we say it. But we are also back to matters of faith. We are to preach what we believe. We actually believe (don't we?) that a social order and an economic order, just like a local community order or a family order, suffused and shaped by solidarity with one another, by generosity towards one another, by doing something for nothing or 'volunteering', by drawing everyone into the action, and tolerating and respecting each other's peculiarities, by sharing what we have – all of which are not the most obvious characteristics of the present global economic order – we actually believe (don't we?) that they are in our self-interest and lead to human happiness and flourishing. This is the Gospel! This is the good news! This is the 'attractiveness of the good' that we should be preaching with all the evangelical fervour and persistence and appetite for conversion we can muster and that we sometimes devote to gospels that are far less true or important. If we are serious about change we have to persuade our generation that its own self-interest is other than it thinks.

Conclusion

As we go out as Christians to campaign on the streets and elsewhere, we should be clear on the following six points and the way they need to go together. First, that God says an absolute 'No' to injustice and poverty. Second, that there are no grounds for demonizing the opposition and arrogating to ourselves the moral high ground: as people we are as bad and as good as each other. Third, that we must say what we are 'for' and not just what we are against. If we judge that the present order won't do we must lobby and campaign for the best alternative we know of, well researched in practice and in theory and drawing on the wisdom of us all. Fourth, we must take full account of the darker side of human nature which will always use power selfishly if it gets the chance, and campaign for measures which distribute power and restrain it. A mere wish-list of ideals will help no one. Fifth, we should frighten people with the consequences of what we are doing as we turn God's earth into a conflictual wasteland which is in nobody's interest at all. Sixth, we should be evangelists for the more attractive possibility we believe in, reflected as it is in the quirky parables of the Bible, where prodigals come home, outsiders become insiders, men do not live by bread alone, the poor become rich, even latecomers get a decent wage, threatening enemies become attractive objects of love, and limited supplies of bread and fish suddenly become more than enough for all.

Finally, we should be clear that we do not campaign for a different order only on 'behalf of' the poor, or 'for' the poor, but 'with' the poor. I have been on quite a few street demonstrations. My favourite of all time was joining a march in Tamil Nadu in South India with about 50 people. Most, but not all, were women. Most, but not all, were landless and poor. All of us were extremely noisy in the best Indian tradition: banging drums, clashing cymbals, blowing whistles, shouting slogans, waving banners, potentially striking the fear of God into everyone who got in our way as we went from field to field demanding change. The demo was against injustice. It was against an economic order that made a few landowners very rich and most people poor. It wanted the redistribution of the land and a more democratic share in the decisions about how it was managed. The protesters went to sit in the house of the rich man to explain how much happier he would be if everyone worked together for the common good. The demo was loud and tough and realistic and self-interested, but with something positive and attractive to say as well. It has not brought in the kingdom as far as I know, but it has changed the face of that part of India where landless people now sit on their land and winnow their harvest in the evening sunshine and can feed their children. They were not Christians as it happened but they were profoundly religious people and they believed in justice and the common good; and they can inspire us and, as it were, go with us as we take, not to the dusty pathways of the Indian countryside, but to the more sophisticated dusty streets of our cities.

5

Rejection or Reform?[1]

When it comes to the global economic order, opinion is divided. Well-meaning people inside the World Bank and the IMF and the governments which control them remain convinced that the present order is alone capable of yielding the economic growth which is fundamental to attaining, for example, the Millennium Development Goals by 2015 and cutting the worst of poverty in half. Meanwhile the poor (and I say this on the back of a recent study in 24 countries[2]) do not believe that the present order will reduce poverty or promote justice and human well-being.

If opinion is divided, criticism of the present order amounts in some cases to outright opposition and hostility. That has been publicly demonstrated in the anti-globalization marches and protests at G8 summit meetings, in slogans such as 'Enough is Enough' and in current talk of a clash of civilizations where one of them is very much identified with global capitalism. Opposition has been expressed more quietly perhaps but equally firmly in many religious movements such as Islam, Buddhism and Hinduism, as I have learned from recent interfaith work on development (as Director of the World Faiths Development Dialogue).[3] Outright opposition is also present within Christian circles. Liberation theology is an obvious example, with its revolutionary approach to redeeming the time; but I think particularly of the European-based Kairos Movement and the writings of Ulrich Duchrow and publications of the World Council

---

[1] A lecture in the UK to the Nottingham Theological Society, October 2003.
[2] See Chapter 3 above.
[3] See Chapter 8 below.

of Churches. One of Duchrow's books is called *Alternatives to Global Capitalism.*[4] A WCC pamphlet of 2001, contemplating encounters with the World Bank and the IMF, is called *Lead Us Not Into Temptation.* And it was from these circles that came the proposal to bracket the economic order with apartheid as a heresy: it is totally incompatible with Christian faith.

Outright opposition of this sort raises questions, at least on the surface, about most of the existing efforts by Christians and others to stand by the world's poor and shape the global economic order to their advantage. The Jubilee Campaign to cancel the debts of the poorest countries and enable them to provide basic healthcare and to send their children to school, is one of them. The Fair Trade campaign to cut out farming subsidies and protection by the rich, allow some protection for the poor, and maximize opportunities for poor countries to sell their goods at reasonable prices, is another. John Dunning, a Christian, has recently edited a book of essays called *Making Globalization Good*[5], by which he means both 'morally good' and 'good for the poor'. The book has much to say about trade and debt but also about the corporate responsibility of transnational corporations and the control of the private and financial sectors.

All these attempts to change things for the better are more radical than simply trying to deal with poverty and inequality through charitable giving and overseas aid and ongoing support for local development projects and programmes. They all go deeper and tackle underlying structural issues. They try to improve the order of things. But they are still a far cry from totally rejecting the whole system and calling for it to be entirely replaced. We might describe them as 'reformist' moves; and it is in the reformist camp that I find myself.

We have, therefore, potentially, two camps, within the Church and beyond it, in the struggle against poverty and injustice as we face up to the powerful vested interest which will maintain the system at all costs, including the cost of military intervention. The two camps may not always eye one another with tolerance and goodwill. Reformists may regard 'rejectionists' as unreasonable,

[4] Ulrich Duchrow, *Alternatives to Global Capitalism* (Utrecht: International Books, 1995).

[5] John Dunning (ed.), *Making Globalization Good* (Oxford: Oxford University Press, 2003).

unrealistic and extreme. Rejectionists may see reformists as compromised, co-opted and wanting to have their cake and eat it by appearing to be on the side of justice while upholding a system which benefits them. Duchrow sees Jesus as firmly in the rejectionist camp, not, of course, of capitalism as we know it today, but of the equally unjust imperial system of his day.[6] Duchrow has also been heavily at odds with his own church in Germany and its support along reformist lines for the social market.[7] All in all, in the struggle against poverty and injustice, it seems possible that divided we may fall.

Recent encounters in WCC circles[8] have raised the following question for me: When it comes to the global economic order, is it a matter of 'rejection' or 'reform' if we are to have integrity as Christian people? The question may not be your question, in which case I apologize. But what follows is the beginnings of an attempt to clear my head: not to answer the question but to look at some of the issues that arise on the way to an answer.

I shall look first at some of the implications of what I have called the rejectionist position; second at whether, in practice, it is so very different from a reformist position; and, to conclude, at ways in which reformists might nevertheless feel challenged by rejectionists.

The rejectionist position: three implications

First, some implications of the rejectionist position. I shall look at three.

1. The first is that the global order is 'all of a piece', so that it is really no good trying to improve or 'reform' a part of it. One thing leads to another. The 'integrity of the economic order' is a little like the 'integrity of creation' much talked about in ecumenical circles. Integrity is full of interconnections. It recognizes the interdependent nature of the whole.

'Globalization' as such is not 'all of a piece', as is sometimes made out. It refers to at least four realities. The first is the increasing interaction between often distant peoples all round the

[6] Duchrow, *Alternatives to Global Capitalism*, p. 189.

[7] Duchrow, *Alternatives to Global Capitalism*, p. 235.

[8] See Rogate R. Mshana (ed.), *Passion for Another World* (Geneva: WCC, 2004).

world. We travel more and more to one another's countries and experience each other's cultures. We trade with each other and buy each other's goods. These phenomena have grown in their significance and intensity in recent times but they are not all that new and not necessarily tied to free market capitalism.

Second is the increasing ease of communication across the globe, not because of travel but because of information technology. Messages, business deals, vast quantities of money, capital and investments can all be sent round the world at a touch on a keyboard. Again, this global reality is not to be wholly identified with free market capitalism. It is of enormous help to capitalism as it moves money across borders but, for example, it can also be an enormous help to its opponents who can be in touch, network and organize their protest marches or email campaigns just as speedily.

A third reality associated with globalization is cultural imperialism. Many fear that unwelcome aspects of Western culture are being imposed on the rest of the world, symbolized by McDonald's and Coca Cola, and more seriously perhaps by the ubiquitous advocacy of 'democracy'. While many apparently accept and welcome these trends, others resist and strenuously reassert their own identities. Again, cultural imperialism is not to be wholly identified with free market capitalism despite the apparent symbiotic relationship between it and democracy. Dominant cultural influences have spread across the world in other periods of history, though once we define the culture as a 'consumer culture' there would seem to be far closer ties between it and the commercial interests of those in the market place who promote it.

A fourth reality brings us nearer to our subject matter, and that is globalization in the form of a global economic order: not the global village, or IT, or Western culture, but what we call free market capitalism. It is 'global' because it is everywhere and touches everybody, even those it studiously leaves out and treats as economic untouchables. But this all-pervasiveness is not what is meant when rejectionists imply that the economic order is all of a piece and that it has to be dealt with as a whole.

Many suggest, for example, that one of the key distortions brought about by free market capitalism is to twist economic activity away from meeting human needs to making and accumulating money and exercising the power that money brings. Two correlates of the distortion are: first, that money ceases to be a convenient means of exchange and becomes what we call a commodity – a thing in itself which can be bought and sold; and, second, the market place ceases to be what we might call a human place, where people meet and exchange goods and services in ways that are mutually beneficial. It becomes instead a place with little if any humanity at all, where money itself, in the form of stocks and shares, is bought and sold to make yet more money and so increase the wealth and influence of those who are already wealthy and influential enough to enter the market in the first place. The profits made in this money market, unlike the profits made in the more human market, are not ploughed back into the business of supplying goods and services and jobs or to provide for those who fall by the wayside. They are used instead to speculate even further and make more money still. When it is implied that the global economic order we call free market capitalism has to be treated in its totality and not piecemeal, this is one thing that is being said: the system is shot through, infected and affected at every turn by this fundamental distortion. It is bent on accumulating money and power rather than meeting human needs. Some have referred to this as the 'god' in the machine (rather than 'the hidden hand'); Jesus might have called it 'Mammon'. To cease to worship this idol involves the wholesale rejection of an integrated system.

A second illustration of the 'integrity' of the economic order comes from a personal experience in Malawi. It can be regarded as representative of a good deal more. In the main street of Lilongwe, the capital, I came across two markets. One was traditional. Traders were sitting on the pavement. What they had to sell was set out in front of them: small piles of tomatoes and vegetables grown on their own plots of land. Next to them was a recently opened branch of Shoprite. It is one of the biggest supermarket chains in southern Africa. I was told that it would rapidly put the street traders out of business since the prices in the supermarket were low and undercut the prices on the street.

Those two adjacent markets focused a range of issues. They illustrated, for example, the interconnection between the more human market meeting human needs and the financial market accumulating money and power. Clearly a supermarket is not a money market but it is directly linked to financial trading and big business which is accountable above all not to its customers but to shareholders. Again, those two markets illustrated how the already powerful benefit from liberalization, or the lifting of controls, so essential to free market capitalism, while the weak go to the wall. Until recently, in Malawi and elsewhere, government-run marketing boards set a guaranteed price for a farmer's produce. There was a safety net through which he could not fall. Those boards have now been removed in favour of open competition. The result has been an influx of cheap products from elsewhere, sold in the supermarkets and making it virtually impossible for the street trader to sell his tomatoes anywhere at all. A street scene in Malawi made the interconnectedness or 'integrity' of the global economy more apparent.

Take another example. Privatization is a lively current debating point. To qualify for debt relief, poor countries are now required to draw up Poverty Reduction Strategies. They must plan in detail how the additional resources released by debt cancellation and any future concessional loans and grants will be used to provide, for example, education and healthcare, clean water and sanitation. Such a strategy will only be funded if it conforms to the economic orthodoxy of the World Bank and the IMF who represent the donors and therefore hold the purse strings. This puts privatization very much on the agenda. The water supply is frequently a candidate. Privatization takes it out of government hands as a public service and puts it in the hands of private companies under contract. On the surface it can look like a sensible piece of pragmatic partnership between the public and private sectors providing investment for the necessary infrastructure, technical know-how, businesslike efficiency and low cost delivery.

Other issues, however, lurk not far beneath the surface. One is a generally negative view of governments and the desire not to build their capacity but to downsize them and reduce their influence, not just over public services but over a nation's economy as a whole. Free market capitalism dislikes government intervention in the market place. Another related issue has to do with opening up the market, at least in theory, to competition in order to stimulate efficient and low cost delivery. I say 'in theory' because in practice there may be very few companies in a position, or willing, to enter the ring. Again, large transnational companies could be eager to bring public services like the water supply under the regulations of the World Trade Organization since in fact it creates a more deregulated situation and allows them easier access than before, unhindered by government intervention.

Two further issues take us back to the 'god' of the system. Many object to the privatization of water because they see water as a primary resource provided by the natural world. It is so basic and essential to human well-being that it can only properly be managed by the community acting together in the interests of all. It is a gift of God. It is not a commodity to be bought and sold. It is for sharing, and not for profit. Again, privatization can be seen as a shift away from meeting human needs to making money. Commercial interests exist primarily to make profits and satisfy shareholders, not to serve people. They certainly do not exist to take on highly unprofitable enterprises which is what supplying water can become. Profits are also made where well-off people can pay their bills, not where people are so poor that they cannot afford to pay anything; where services are quickly installed and easily maintained, not in remote village communities.

The rejectionist position implies not only an all-pervasive system which touches so many aspects of our lives but a tightly interlocking system shot through at every point with the same basic distortion, not to say perversion, of what an economic order should be about. Hence their descriptions of it as 'closed' and 'totalitarian'[9] and their conviction that mere reform is not enough. We must question the system as a whole.

2. A second implication of the rejectionist position, especially as articulated by Christians, is that the free market system in their judgment is inextricably wedded to values that are contrary to Christian faith. It embodies them; it is inspired by them; and it could not survive without them. Two examples are: debt and competition.

For centuries the Christian tradition was hostile to usury or the lending of money with interest. Rightly or wrongly there is no great hostility towards it today. We can even cite some highly constructive current examples of it which appear to be on the side of justice rather than exploitation, such as credit unions which lend money to poor people – often women – who would otherwise never have access to bank loans. They use the money to cope with family crises such as illness or funerals, or to build a house, or start a business. The rate of interest is low and it is used not to make a money lender

---

[9] See Duchrow, *Alternatives to Global Capitalism*, pp. 122–3, 193.

rich but to build up the resources to make more loans to help more people. The Grameen Bank in Bangladesh is perhaps the largest financial institution in the world (in contrast to the many small local co-operatives) which is run along these lines.

Lending money with interest for social purposes may well then be compatible with Christian values. The sequence of events which led to the international debt crisis can be seen in this light. Originally, it could be argued, loans were made to poor countries to assist them in their development. In other words, they were made for social purposes. Was it, however, the underlying motive? At the time, besides the fear of a looming financial crisis, Western banks had money to burn in the form of petro-dollars. It could not lie idle. The money had to be set to work, not primarily for the benefit of the poor, but to make more money for the bank's shareholders and investors. Hence the sudden interest in the developing world. The loan agreements subsequently made between banks and governments were often ill-advised. Countries not in a position to manage large amounts of money were encouraged nevertheless to accept them. An already irre-sponsible situation then turned into a crisis for a number of reasons. One was corruption and mismanagement. The loans generated no new resources or economic growth to benefit either poor or rich but went into the pockets of dictators and a powerful elite. Another reason for the crisis was the fall in price of the one or two commodities, like coffee, which poor countries had to sell on the world market. A third cause of the disaster was a rise in interest rates to protect the economies of rich countries, including the USA. Faced with falling incomes and rising interest rates, poor countries were forced to borrow more in order to make the repayments on their original loan. So their indebtedness increased. Irresponsible lending and borrowing then turned into the unsustainable debts of poor countries now known as highly indebted poor countries – HIPCs: unsustainable because they could not afford to service them. Instead of furthering social purposes the system worked against them. Poor countries had to choose between providing education and healthcare for their people on the one hand and repaying their debts on the other. Those who had not been party to the original agreements – the people themselves – were made to suffer unjustly the conse-quences of what their governments and Western bankers had done.

Was all this – and is all this, since the debt crisis is far from over – an unfortunate blip in an otherwise satisfactory economic system, or does it all reflect a set of values which are intrinsic to the system itself: the oxygen without which it cannot live? Is the debt crisis a bad accident or is it inevitable?

It was often argued by banks and then by the international financial institutions, when debt became largely the problem of multinational agencies like the World Bank and the IMF, that if debts were cancelled and not repaid the whole system would no longer work: a reminder of its dependence on the sanctity of contracts. But free market capitalism not only requires that debts should be repaid but that debts should be created. If money is to make more money, it has to be invested and it has to make profits. The deliberate creation of debt is what drives the economy and it is that which is said to be unacceptable to Christian faith and discipleship. It is not a form of usury which pursues social purposes but a form of usury which pursues profit.

Another value often seen to be incompatible with Christian teaching is competition. Again there are more superficial and more fundamental issues involved. Even in what we might call the human market place, where goods and services are exchanged for the mutual benefit of all, two forms of competition will nevertheless take place. People will try to outdo one another in the quality of the goods they produce. Initiative and hard work will to some extent be rewarded. A certain amount of rivalry will ensure that standards are high. Again, the market is a reasonably effective exchange mechanism matching needs and supplies, so that needs will compete with one another as well as skills. Some goods and services will gain a competitive edge because they are needed more. Competition, therefore, need not be wholly ruled out or seen as totally hostile to co-operation.

More fundamentally, however, it is argued, free market capitalism does not merely contain healthy competitive elements; it is competitive by nature. Various enterprises compete for attention. The least risky and most successful are bound to attract the most resources. Investors, so-called, look for high returns on capital at low risk. Success then breeds success. Wealth and power are increasingly concentrated. The poor are increasingly left out of the running, unable to compete with the attractiveness of the rich. That is the way the system works; and in so far as it is cut-throat and 'beggar-your-neighbour', not mutually beneficial, it is inimical to Christian faith and discipleship.

Similarly negative remarks can be made about consumption. There are plenty of warnings in the Christian tradition about allowing it to get out of control. In the gospels we have the memorable example of the lilies of the field along with the advice to seek first the kingdom and let material considerations find their own level. Free market capitalism, in stark contrast, depends on creating needs and stimulating consumption in order to maintain economic growth. If we don't consume more and more the economy will grind to a halt.

Turning to the environment, Christian attitudes were somewhat distorted by the Enlightenment and the scientific rationalism which objectified nature and encouraged us to read into biblical passages, like the early stories of Genesis, a mandate for exploiting the earth. Now Christianity teaches us to be careful stewards of nature, managing and conserving its resources for the well-being of all living creatures and future generations. But the free market economy, it is argued, has an appetite for natural resources which nature can never satisfy. In order to consume more and more we make more and more and in the course of doing so we pollute, destroy and exhaust the environment.

Beyond all this, according to rejectionists, the core value of the economy, inimicable to Christian faith, remains the fact that it subordinates people to the system, and in two ways. First, the most significant market places of the world – the financial markets – no longer serve the needs of people but aim to multiply money and power. Second, control of the economy is no longer in the hands of the people it is meant to serve. The markets are not subject to local or national democratic and participatory political systems. At best they are self-regulating or out of control. At worst they themselves have turned on us, as it were, and now rule the world. The economy is no longer made for man, but man for the economy.

So the second implication of the rejectionist position is that free market capitalism only survives by promoting values such as usury, competition, consumption, the subjugation of nature and people, which are contrary to Christian faith and teaching and, it might be added, by undermining values such as human solidarity and co-operation, which are not.

3. A third implication can be dealt with more briefly. We can assume, I take it, that all Christians everywhere reject abject involuntary material poverty without question. The fact that almost half the world's population lives on less than two dollars a day and one fifth on less than one dollar and that 840 million people are officially classified as malnourished[10] – that millions have scarcely enough to survive on, let alone really 'live', or feed their families or educate their children – finds no support in anybody's Christian faith and teaching. Here everyone stands with the rejectionists without further debate. Poverty of that kind is not a Christian value. Voluntary poverty is, of course, another matter.

That, however, is not quite the point. The third implication of the rejectionist position is not that capitalists necessarily approve of poverty (some in practice apparently do, since they do little to alleviate it, but many don't and, like Bill Gates and George Soros and others, appear to work hard to be rid of it). No, the implication is not that capitalists value poverty but that the capitalist system inevitably produces it. It is essentially an engine of poverty.

Whether poverty overall has increased or decreased under free market capitalism is highly debatable. Once again, views differ and the evidence is decidedly mixed. For example, although the rise of modern capitalism in the West, along with the industrial revolution, initially brought misery to many industrial workers, in time millions of people in Europe and North America rose out of poverty to enjoy a vastly higher standard of living. Capitalism, it could be argued, made them rich – so why should it not make others rich? On the other hand, the cost of that achievement was borne by faraway peoples whose primary products and labour were had on the cheap and who were not allowed to share in the more lucrative manufacturing activities of the economic system. So capitalism made some rich and others poor. In modified forms, however, it has raised living standards even in poorer countries. The Asian Tigers, who did not obey all the rules associated with the so-called 'Washington Consensus' but still operated on broadly capitalist lines, are a case in point. Again, when it comes to crunching numbers the news is not all bad. The global economic order can still chalk up some promising statistics in some parts of the world with regard to falling infant mortality

---

[10] See George Monbiot, *The Age of Consent* (London: Flamingo, 2003), p. 17.

rates, rising numbers of children going to school, higher per capita incomes, greater availability of potable water: all standard measures of material poverty and wealth. Some of these statistics can be highly misleading, of course. Higher per capita incomes as an average figure can mask disparities within a country and the increased costs of, say, school fees and healthcare can more than cancel out apparent gains. It cannot be denied, however, that some statistics move significantly in the right direction. When it comes to the persistence of poverty, Africa is often seen as the worst case scenario, blighted by hunger and war and lack of investment. The evidence suggests that free market capitalism has done it very little good at all. Some of its leading rulers, however, in signing up for NEPAD (the New Economic Partnership for African Development) apparently believe that, in spite of everything, free market capitalism is their best hope of turning Africa's economic fortunes around. It can be an ally in the fight against poverty. By way of contrast, material poverty is once again becoming problematic in the so-called North as a social problem on a significant scale; and the poor are not just the strangers within our gates: the migrants and immigrants. The evidence, then, that free market capitalism is inevitably linked to poverty creation and not just wealth creation, is mixed.

Maybe the third implication of the rejectionist position is better put in another way. It is certainly not true that all capitalists are in favour of poverty, and it is not at all clear that free market capitalism inevitably breeds poverty rather than gradually improving living standards through economic growth and its trickle-down effects. It seems far more plausible to suggest that what it inevitably does lead to is growing disparities between rich and poor. It widens the gap and drives a wedge between people so that, if the poor are not quite so poor as they were, the rich are even richer and the differences between them more and more obvious and resented. Why should this be inevitable? The answers lie in the driven nature of the system as it accumulates money and power, in its emphasis on wealth creation rather than wealth distribution and, above all, in its competitive nature. Capitalism can only succeed if it minimizes risks and invests resources not in the poor where they are most needed, but in the rich who have already proved themselves successful. The precise implication, then, is not that capitalism inevitably makes people poor but that it is intrinsically divisive. It goes against all that Christians believe about human equality (in the sense that we are all equally important) and about human solidarity (in the sense that we are not essentially rivals). We are called, not to disregard each other's interests in a cut-throat race to succeed, but to love our neighbour and be the keeper of our brothers and sisters in mutual service.

We have looked at three implications of the rejectionist position. The global economic order is all of a piece. It cannot survive unless inspired by values inimical to Christian faith and teaching. It inevitably widens the gap between rich and poor and drives us apart. My present purpose is not to ask whether this analysis is correct, though it is certainly not beyond criticism! I myself would question, for example, the picture of a tightly closed system, interlocking, thoroughly coherent, interdependent, internally consistent and 'all of a piece'. It is doubtful that human beings could ever produce such a thing. It seems more like the work of a god than of men. And, as we have seen, there is evidence that modifications have been made to the system as well as departures from, say, the Washington Consensus without the capitalist system in general being brought to its knees. Economic reality is more subtle and complex than this picture makes out. Again, although the power accumulated by wealth can be extremely oppressive, history suggests it does not totally over-whelm the less powerful or exclude the rise of opposing forces (as at present in the so-called war against terrorism or in the new alliances within the World Trade Organization). The result can be power struggles rather than a simple monopoly of power.

But my purpose is not to ask whether the rejectionists are correct in their analysis but to ask whether in fact they are so very different from the reformers, especially when it comes to deciding what action to take in favour of the poor and human solidarity, and out of respect for the natural world and its resources.

Rejectionists in practice

Here I want to make two sets of remarks.

1. The first is about alternatives to the global economic order. Capitalists have famously remarked that 'there is no alternative' (TINA) to capitalism in the aftermath of the collapse of the socialist economies. The rejectionists, on the other hand, are challenged to produce one, and are often criticized for being

highly dismissive of the existing order while have nothing to put in its place. This criticism is not entirely fair. Not having all the answers to a problem immediately to hand hardly precludes us from recognizing that a problem exists. Those who reject free market capitalism, however, insist that they do have constructive proposals to make.

During discussion at a recent WCC meeting one speaker declared: 'There are a thousand alternatives'.[11] Ulrich Duchrow publishes a long list of examples.[12] They include the 'small is beautiful' philosophy of Schumacher; the environmentalist focus on sustainability;[13] the centrality of respect for the land of the eco-feminists; the declaration of the Social Forum and the work of the New Economics Foundation.

One alternative, much discussed, is 'localization' which, crudely speaking, suggests that the resources of a locality (e.g. a nation or region, even a metropolis) should be used first and foremost within it.[14] These could be natural resources, or the resources of agricultural production, or the skills of its people. Goods and services which can be produced locally *should* be, in contrast to the way in which goods and services are transported vast distances across the globe. In its most rigorous form, 'localization' could be questioned for insulating and isolating localities and communities from the outside world in a way which is now impossible in the face of globalization and is in any case undesirable since it would lead to another set of unjust outcomes where one locality's resources are more than enough to meet its needs while another's are not sufficient at all. This, however, is to overlook the complementary concept of 'internationalism' (in contrast to globalization) where knowledge, technology and resources are shared across borders in order to build up the sustainability of local economies elsewhere to the eventual benefit of everyone. 'Localization', as a bias or rule of thumb, could be seen as an economic version of 'subsidiarity': of not doing at the global level what can be done at a more local level. In other words, 'act locally' unless other considerations, such as the shortage of basic

---

[11] See note 8 above.

[12] Duchrow, *Alternatives to Global Capitalism*, p. 24.

[13] Carefully worked out by Peter Soderbaum in Mshana (ed.), *Passion for Another World*, Ch. 4

[14] See, for example, Monbiot, *The Age of Consent* and Colin Hines, *Localisation – A Global Manifesto* (London: Earthscan, 2000).

resources and opportunities in one place and their abundance in another, suggest otherwise. Understood in this way, 'localization', it is claimed, can deal with some of the fundamental failings and distortions of free market capitalism. It can focus back on meeting the needs of people where people have a better chance of being in control instead of being dictated to by powerful external institutions whose interests are largely financial and elsewhere. It can help environmentalists in reducing the distances goods are transported – with all the attendant costs, pollution and environmental damage. 'Localization' also opens the door to something other than a 'one size fits all' economy where cultural differences can be respected and find expression.

The complaint, then, that rejectionists know what they're against but don't know what they are for is not entirely fair. There are alternatives, even if as yet they are not high in the public consciousness. A number of questions remain, however. For example, do these proposals add up to an alternative 'global', or comprehensive, economic order, capable of ordering the global interconnections of trade and commerce from which we can hardly now escape, in ways that are just and sustainable? 'Localization', for example, for which I have some sympathy, is in one sense a global alternative in that it is to be applied everywhere, but it seems less convincing at present when describing how each locality (national or regional) should relate or interact with all the others. Its 'trade rules', for example, to replace the existing rules of the World Trade Organization, seem somewhat unwieldy and impractical (though maybe no more so than the existing ones!). Or, again, some proposals (about co-operatives or appropriate technology, for example) are little more than experimental fragments: partial answers but not the whole. Sometimes all we appear to have are principles on which an acceptable economic order should be based but stopping far short of being embodied in actual economic policies. Some will ask whether the alternative to free market capitalism should ever be 'global' in any case, if it is to avoid the totalitarianism of state-centred socialist economies on the one hand and of free market capitalism holding everything in its vicelike grip and dictated by a minority of interests on the other. Is not the proper alternative a plurality of economic orders suited to different places, peoples and cultures? (An Islamic writer in Dunning's book on *Making Globalization Good*, already referred to, recently argued in this way.[15]) But even if so, a 'global economic order' still has to be established so that different economies, whether marked by localism or pluralism, can happily live side by side and, where necessary, relate to one another.

Two further questions might be asked about the search for alternatives. When is an alternative simply a thoroughgoing reform, bringing the financial markets under political control, for example, or instituting a negative interest rate on accumulated wealth; and when is the reform so drastic that the consequences are different in kind and not simply of degree?

Again, if there are alternatives, how in practice is the existing order (or disorder) of free market capitalism to be replaced: the old order by the new? How are we to move from where we are to where we want to be? Short of revolution on a global scale, and George Monbiot encourages such a move in the form of a threat by all highly indebted countries to 'dump' their debts and refuse to pay them,[16] it is hard to envisage anything other than a gradualist approach to change. If that is so, then rejectionists may not be so very different in practice from reformists, and debt and trade campaigns may be efforts round which both can unite.

2. The second set of remarks is about what rejectionists actually propose to do to change the economic order for the better. The answers, organized under four headings, are not necessarily theirs: Prophesying, Taming, Experimenting and Networking. Little more need be said under the heading of 'Prophesying'. Rejectionists are fundamentally opposed to the system. They, like an Amos, are thereby confrontational. They utter the prophetic 'No'. Free market capitalism is thoroughly unacceptable in the name of God and of humanity. Rejectionists are opposed in principle and repeatedly say so, loud and clear.

Nevertheless, there can still be a willingness to look at particular aspects of the system. They seem prepared to negotiate as well as to confront, as if there is an agenda recognized by both sides which is worth addressing. Such negotiations have been described as attempts to *tame* the system. The report of a recent WCC consultation illustrates the point.[17] It was called in September 2003 to prepare for future meetings between the Christian

---

[15] Khurshid Ahmad in Dunning, *Making Globalization Good*, pp. 181–209.

[16] Monbiot, *The Age of Consent*, p. 176.

[17] The report is unpublished, but see Mshana (ed.), *Passion for Another World*.

ecumenical church family and representatives of the World Bank and the International Monetary Fund. A prophetic note was struck. The existing economic order continues to damage the poor and widen the disparities between them and the rich, and it is contrary in all sorts of ways to Christian belief and practice. There can be no compromise here and no discussion except on their terms, which are not judged to be the terms of the Bank and the Fund. The same document, however, goes on to itemize three issues which the World Council of Churches is prepared to raise with the Bank and the Fund when they next meet. One is people's participation, especially in the Poverty Reduction Strategy Processes in poor countries, where money released by cancelling debts is supposed to be used according to the people's priorities and in their interests. The second is the accountability of institutions like the Bank and the Fund and ensuring that they are governed in a way that more fairly represents the interests of poorer countries. A third issue has to do with 'privatization' and what might be the legitimate and complementary roles of governments and the private sector in poverty reduction and development. The privatization of public services, like the water supply, is of particular concern.

Attempts to improve aspects of the system rather than change the system completely can therefore apparently be justified. Nobody believes we can have the new world of a just and sustainable order all at once, or inherit the kingdom tomorrow. Nothing less than fundamental, structural change may be necessary, but achieving it is a long and hazardous journey. What is to happen to the poorest of the poor in the meantime? Many will be born and die. It is only responsible, not to say loving towards our neighbours, to act sooner and not just later to improve some matters. The perfect cannot be allowed to become the enemy of the good. Rejectionists, arguing in this way, appear, therefore, to accept the need for interim measures to tame the system or try to draw the worst of its sting. Debt reform and trade reform, both of which leave the underlying order in place, would be examples.

Colin Hines in his debate with George Monbiot about 'localisation' (neither arguing explicitly on Christian grounds) is critical of 'taming' the system. He writes:

the politically active ... must shift from just fighting separate issues-specific aspects of globalisation to realising that their individual successes can only be secured as part of an overarching change ... What is occurring at present is an array of well meaning, pragmatic, but inevitably limited efforts by political activists ... to tame globalisation. Campaigns for 'labour standards' or 'fair trade' or 'voluntary ethical codes' fundamentally mistake the nature of the ... beast. These attempts are like trying to lasso a tiger with cotton.[18]

Nevertheless, as we shall see, Hines is prepared to tackle aspects of the system rather than everything at once, so long as a gradualist or piecemeal approach is made coherent within an overall strategy.

Third, if opposition to the global economic order is to be constructive, some *experimenting* needs to be done. Many experiments will be relatively small scale but capable of being multiplied. Other experiments will be pieces of a jigsaw which, put together, could make up a more satisfying whole. Examples would include localized economies, co-operatives, sustainable agriculture, environmental taxation and life-styles embodying the Christian principles and values which the present order is seen to violate.

If these experiments often seem utopian and fail to take account of the less constructive ways human beings tend to behave, a fourth and final set of actions introduces a note of realism. I have called it *networking*. It recognizes that issues of power are fundamental. The present economic system is in the hands of powerful vested interests, both financial and political. They are unlikely to change willingly what reaps such benefits for themselves. They are even more unlikely to cede power to the critics of free market capitalism. Countervailing powers have therefore to be built up so that scattered pockets of protest and experiment become coherent forces which in the end can effectively challenge the existing order. The World Social Forum and the internationalizing of the Jubilee Campaign on debt and the campaign on trade could be examples of that. The new alliance formed at the World Trade Organization meetings in Cancun, 2003, bringing China and India and many of the poorer countries into united opposition, illustrate just how problematic networking can be. In the long run their interests may be very

---

[18] Colin Hines, unpublished review of Monbiot's *The Age of Consent*, pp. 14–15.

different. Having united on this particular issue, they may soon be divided as South–South competitors, formed in the image of a system that remains basically unchanged.

This quick cataloguing of actions taken by rejectionists suggests that many of them are not all that different from actions taken by those who see themselves as reformists and remain genuinely at a loss to imagine what an alternative global economy might look like. Rejectionist efforts to tame the system, for example, are in fact quite similar to reformist campaigns on debt and trade. Both look for debt cancellation. Both look for fairer prices and an end to subsidies which simply damage a fragile economy in another part of the world. Again, rejectionist 'experiments' have some similarities to development projects and programmes promoted by NGOs and others who are very much in the reformist camp. Both encourage co-operation rather than competition; both increase participation by communities and their control over what is happening to them. The importance of networking in order to build strong and coherent movements for change is recognized by reformers and rejectionists alike.

Conclusion

Let me make four sets of remarks in conclusion.

1. First, in the light of this rather preliminary discussion, I tend to think that, at least in practice, there is not a great deal of difference between those who completely reject and those who try to reform the global economic order. Both are adamant that increasing or maintaining poverty and creating ever widening gaps between rich and poor are unacceptable to a proper understanding of Christian faith and teaching. And both set about reversing the situation in much the same way. They protest. They try to improve parts of the system in favour of the poor. They support different and, for them, more acceptable ways of doing things, and among both rejectionists and reformers are those who are clear-eyed about the realities of power.

2. Second, even if rejectionists look much the same as reformers in practice, what challenges might they nevertheless represent? I can think of two. One I am acutely aware of in my work with the World Faiths Development Dialogue. Part of our mandate is to promote dialogue on development not only between the different

faith communities (Christian, Muslim, Buddhist, Hindu, etc.) seeing where they can join hands in common endeavour, but also between those communities and multilateral agencies like the World Bank: a development agency which has met with more suspicion than trust from local, grass roots religious communities all round the world. In particular we are seeing how the work of faith communities in poverty reduction and development can be scaled up with financial help from the World Bank to maximize their contributions to the United Nations 2015 targets or the Millennium Development Goals. The World Bank seems keen to bring these faith communities, as they gather round their mosques, churches and temples, and as they engage in education and healthcare and the struggle against HIV/AIDS, into this grand endeavour to cut the worst of the world's poverty in half in just ten years' time. 'Bringing them on board', however, raises some difficult questions. I mention only one. How far is this process, technically referred to in Bank circles as 'scaling-up', a genuine attempt at co-operation in a common cause; and how far is it a matter of being co-opted into an approach to development heavily committed to economic growth and structural adjustment about which we have fundamental reservations? We cannot be against co-operation and we cannot be against poverty reduction, but on whose terms do we co-operate, and are religious communities being drawn into strategies which, at a more fundamental level, they actually oppose? Instead of even taming the tiger are we riding the tiger? The rejectionists, who would I assume tend to stop at active co-operation of this kind (much to the perplexity, as I have observed, of World Bank staff who seem to assume that ideologies are not at stake here or not relevant when it comes to tackling urgent practical problems) can help to maintain in Christian people and others a healthy self-awareness and a proper level of unease. The rejectionists can make an important contribution as they police the demarcation lines between co-operation with all people of goodwill for the common good and co-option into policies and practices which will do the world's poor little good at all.

3. A second contribution of the rejectionists may be to constantly challenge us to go deep enough in our analysis and our reactions to the global economic order. We know that world poverty cannot be dealt with purely by emergency aid and charitable giving. We know that it is not sufficient, however

necessary, to support discrete development projects and programmes. We know there has to be structural change, and that is
why the churches and their agencies have turned in recent years
to advocacy and campaigning on issues like trade and debt. These
efforts, however, might still stop short of getting to the root of the
problem. The cancellation of the debts of the poorest countries
can leave the system which created the crisis in the first place
largely untouched. Better rules of trade and an end to agriculture
subsidies may not touch the financial markets. In other words,
stopping at this level, the show may well go on. The rejectionists
may be wrong in seeing the global economy as 'all of a piece',
where you cannot tackle the problems it creates without tackling
the whole; but they may well be right when they insist that there is
a god in this economic machine, or an all-pervasive perverted
spirit, and that if we fail to dethrone the god and exorcize the
spirit, or root out this fundamental perversion, we shall in the
long run achieve little. At least we must make sure that our various
campaigns on debt, trade, the environment, democracy, the arms
trade or whatever, are all of a piece and firmly linked and
contribute to progress on two fundamental issues. One is the way
in which the economy is run to accumulate money and power
rather than human needs. The other is the way in which it is out of
the control of the people it is meant to serve. If our debt and trade
and environmental campaigns don't contribute to turning round
these two root perversions – putting people first and restoring
their control of the economic order – then we might not even be
reformers but those who, by advocating limited change, perpetuate systems rather than redeem them.

If free market capitalist policies cohere round very clear aims
which have to do with making money and increasing power, so
must the campaigns of those who oppose them. Colin Hines in
advocating 'localization' is against 'taming' the system,[19] but the
steps he takes remain inevitably piecemeal, whether on protective
trade barriers, environmental taxation or the transfer of technology. These discrete actions are, however, firmly located within an
overall coherent strategy and in that sense are not piecemeal at
all.

4. Finally, posing questions about 'reform' or 'rejection' and
'reform' or 'replacement' when it comes to tackling the global

---

[19] Hines, unpublished review of Monbiot, *The Age of Consent*, p. 13.

economic order might turn out to be useful as an analytic tool. Such questions may help us to be clearer: about the realities we are dealing with (is it a totalitarian system, for example, or a more complex and open order?); about the options open to us (is it wiping the slate clean in a revolutionary way or gradually changing things for the better?); and about the steps we can take, from prophetic to strategic.

It might also be fruitful and interesting to see how this 'analytic' tool relates to other analytic tools or ways of understanding how opinions vary and divide. We have talked about rejectionists and reformers. We could also talk about 'principled and pragmatic' approaches, and 'utopians and realists' and, as a matter of fact, 'rich and poor'. Above all is the classic typology of 'church-type' and 'sect-type' elaborated by Ernst Troeltsch and built on by Richard Niebuhr in his classic book: *Christ and Culture*[20] where at first glance rejectionists and reformers might be thought to echo the two types of 'church' and 'sect' or 'Christ against Culture' and 'Christ the Reformer of Culture'. That, however, would be misleading.

The rejectionists we have been talking about are not against culture as such, in the way Niebuhr understood it. They are not among those who wish to withdraw from or reject worldly affairs altogether. They are against a particular culture: the culturally constructed global economic system we call free market capitalism. The danger with reformists is that they easily fall into the third of Niebuhr's six types, namely that of 'Christ of Culture' where the one too easily conforms to and embraces the other. Christian capitalists clearly do so. The reformers of capitalism may also do so if the changes they propose are not radical enough because the problems of the economy are far more deep-seated than they appear to acknowledge.

One final observation. These discussions about reforming and rejecting the global economic order are in one way deeply theological or ideological. They are about the ways in which economic systems promote and embody certain beliefs about human beings and the world around them and what really matters. They raise issues about our values and what we worship. But in another way these discussions are not very theological at all. They are about which economic system might best bring about an

---

[20] Richard Niebuhr, *Christ and Culture* (London: Faber, 1952).

agreed aim. The aim is a sustainable economy that meets our needs and allows us all to flourish. Whether it is brought about by a modified form of capitalism, such as the social market, or by increasing 'localization', whether by re-empowering national governments or redesigning international institutions or both, is largely a matter of what I would call socio-economic technology. This underlines a point which Ronald Preston[21] and others of his generation were keen to stress: that while 'science', whether social science or economics, is never value-free, and theology remains an essential discipline, we should never allow the latter to think more highly of itself than it ought to think. As Christians, if we are serious about finding alternatives to an economic order that betrays our faith, we probably need the economists and social scientists as much if not more than the theologians in the present phase of our explorations.

[21] See p. 4 and Chapter 6.

6

Faith in the Global Economic System[1]

My title is ambiguous. Clearly it raises the issue of confidence in the global system, especially in its ability to deliver the goods: both material and moral. Have we got any faith in it? A recent study in 24 countries suggests that the world's poor have little confidence that the system will ever work for them.[2] Members of Western governments, including our own, publicly committed to reducing world poverty, disagree. They point to some improving statistics. They declare that poor countries need more economic globalization, not less, and can trade their way out of poverty. Despite Enron and September 11th and volatile financial markets, the Managing Director of the International Monetary Fund still proclaims the resilience of the capitalist system,[3] while the World Bank insists that the Poverty Reduction Strategies of the poorest countries must conform to existing macroeconomic and structural adjustment policies if they are to be funded and if they are to succeed. Opinion remains divided, with opposition amounting to fury at one extreme (where some Christians have described the system as heresy) and commitment amounting to evangelical fervour at the other. I shall return briefly to this issue of confidence at the end of the chapter.

My ambiguous title also reflects a concern which dominated so much of Ronald Preston's life and work. He wanted to ensure that

---

[1] One of the Samuel Ferguson Lectures in the University of Manchester, UK in 2003. First published in *The Future of Christian Social Ethics. A Special Issue of Studies in Christian Ethics*, 17/2 (2004), pp. 197–215.

[2] Taylor, *Christianity, Poverty and Wealth*, p. 14.

[3] For example in a speech in Berlin, 15 November 2002.

our Christian faith not only motivated and supported us in our efforts to create an economic order that worked for everyone, but also played its part in shaping and informing the substance of our economic policies; that they were not devoid of the insights of faith; that not only Christian people but Christian convictions, both theological and ethical, were 'inside' or an integral part of the system. It was this concern which led Preston: to search the scriptures and tradition; to reject any over-direct moves from doctrine to economic policy; to worry about the limits to what the Church as Church could say; to respect empirical data; to talk (and then to stop talking!) about 'middle axioms'; to acknowledge the autonomy of other disciplines and the need to work with them; and to believe that principled policy agreements could be reached across differences because of our shared human experience and rationality.

Preston was well aware of the complexities involved in getting faith into the social and economic orders, or doing social theology. He has been criticized, however, though here he may have been no more than a child of his time, for underestimating plurality. He failed, it is said, to recognize fully the great gulf fixed between different moral systems, rooted as they are in the different stories or narratives we tell in our communities as we attempt to understand our lives. He was insufficiently aware of his own partiality and his tendency to universalize the rational or reasonable Christian tradition in which he stood. He underestimated the competence or 'expertise' of unsophisticated witnesses and the need to deal seriously with their divergent views. He overestimated the extent of the fundamental human experience which all of us share despite our differences, and its potential when searching for agreement.

Preston was quite capable of replying to his critics[4] whom he regarded as taking postmodernism a step too far, even a dangerous step if pluralism finally meant that, since we virtually inhabit different worlds, there is no point in talking morality to each other or even talking to each other at all – a conclusion which argumentative pluralists and postmodernists thankfully seem reluctant to reach.

Pluralism, however, remains the ever-present context in which many of us have to work, including those like me who work in

[4] See R. John Elford and Ian S. Markham (eds.), *The Middle Way* (London: SCM Press, 2000), pp. 210–11.

poverty reduction and human development and try to incorporate the insights of religious faith into social and economic policy and practice. I want first to underline some familiar features of pluralism and then suggest how we should respond to it and describe the nature of any agreements we might reach.

Three features of plurality

First, it is multi-faith. Almost all of Ronald Preston's endeavours in the field of social theology can be classed as 'Christian' social theology (which is not to say he was unaware of other faith traditions). But in contemporary debates about poverty and development, if we are going to talk about faith in the forums that matter, we can no longer bring only one faith to the table. For example, with the Millennium Development Goals in mind we ask about the nature of human development where all the emphasis seems to be on economic development to the neglect of its social and cultural aspects. We try to engage with current issues like the World Bank's World Development Report 2004 (WDR 2004) on *Making Services* [like education and healthcare] *Work for Poor People*. We try to reshape or moderate the global economy in favour of a more equitable distribution of resources and opportunities and benefits. We work for debt cancellation and poverty reduction in some of the world's poorest countries. In all of this we try to argue and act as people of faith bringing that faith to bear on the issues; but since the issues are global we can no longer act simply as Christians or assume that, once we have contributed our Christian insights, the work of faith is done. Our Christian insights have to engage with those of other faiths before conclusions can be reached. The result is a plurality scarcely touched on in a great deal of Christian social thinking. Even if we are prepared to dismiss their validity, we cannot dismiss the existence of other faiths and their influence. They are players that have to be reckoned with. And it is not just a matter of the plurality of faiths: Christianity, Islam, Buddhism, Judaism, Hinduism, Sikhism, and so forth. It is also a matter of plurality within each faith tradition[5], brought home to me, for example, yet again when I met not only with Sunnis or Shiites in Albania but

---

[5] See the typology in Taylor, *Christianity, Poverty and Wealth*, pp. 27–34.

with Becktashi, a fascinating Islamic sect with strong Christian elements dating from the days of the Ottoman Empire together with angrier Muslim influences coming in and financed by Saudi Arabia; and finding in Ghana that the various expressions of Islam were almost as numerous as those of Christianity. How do all these 'faiths' get into the economic system?

A second feature of contemporary plurality can be highlighted by referring to two current arguments within the development community, a community which includes huge agencies like the World Bank, the IMF and the UK's Department for International Development (DFLD), alongside NGOs like Christian Aid and Islamic Relief, civil society and faith communities like churches, mosques and temples. The World Bank and the IMF are frequently accused of peddling a 'one size fits all' solution to the economic ills of poor communities (though the draft WDR 2004 speaks of '12 sizes'). Structural Adjustment Policies are one example and the macroeconomic policies, to which Poverty Reduction Strategies are expected to conform, are another. They are regarded by many as the same old SAPs by any other name. They require poor countries: to open up their markets to the outside world; to lower trade barriers; to give a more significant role to the private sector in providing social services like water and sanitation; and generally to reduce the role of the state. It is an all-encompassing global economic view from above.

The language of DFLD takes on a similar flavour when it talks about 'the big picture'. It has grown impatient with relatively small-scale, unrelated and unstrategic development projects and the NGOs which have funded them. It is strongly biased in favour of turning around weak, corrupt and ineffective governments so that they can deliver co-ordinated programmes of education and healthcare on the massive scale required.

These grand scenarios involving global policies and government-to-government actions certainly have their place. But they tend to be dismissive of much more untidy realities on the ground which world banks and governments are not always well placed to deal with. In one East African country, for example, government programmes don't reach outlying villages, and no one reports the fact, because District Officers will never travel further afield than a day's return journey. In one Asian country health education programmes make little progress because of the traditional cultural relations between men and women. HIV/

AIDS, on the other hand, makes rapid progress for similar reasons. In many societies handouts to your own people, far from being seen as corrupt practice, are only to be expected of upright leaders of communities where extended family loyalties come first. Women in an African village broke the pumps that delivered water to their doorsteps because they resented being robbed of the time it took to fetch and carry water together: their only chance to talk and sing. Sitting recently with IMF officials I heard reports from leaders of faith communities in Malawi as to how and why their people were short of food. The evidence was in contrast to the statistical overview put forward by the World Food Programme. Their reports were described and also dismissed as 'anecdotal'.

This is but a tiny sampling of the myriad, untidy grass roots realities which refuse to fit easily into the 'big picture' or respond to universal solutions. In this sense the world is stubbornly plural rather than singular.

Ronald Preston got into more than one tetchy argument during his long and distinguished career. One was with the World Council of Churches, and one aspect of it was his scepticism of the increasing respect being shown to what 'the people' rather than 'the experts' had to say. It was a swing away from what some ecumenical pundits at the time regarded as the elitist approach of more traditional ecumenical social thinking to which Preston had contributed so much. It was not for Westerners with their oppressive rationalism and their expertise to presume to know best or better than ordinary, everyday people on the ground. Characteristically, Preston does not dismiss the point entirely. Everyday people, 'lay people' and poor people have of course a right to be heard and have much of value to contribute. But, like the postmodernists, he judged that the new ecumenists were in danger of going too far. There was now too much respect for what the people had to say and a romantic reluctance to admit that they could be as wrong as anybody else: their relative ignorance on the technical front, for example, was not necessarily bliss. More interesting for my present purpose was Preston's insistence that it was misleading to refer to what 'the people' said because 'the people', including the poor and oppressed, who were of such central importance to the liberation theologians, were not a homogeneous group. They didn't say the same thing. Like the experts, they were often disagreeing among themselves.

Here then is a second, in my view striking, feature of contemporary plurality. The first is the plurality of faiths, varied among and within themselves. The second is the untidy plurality of particular places, communities, cultures and peoples on the ground, with their differences and idiosyncrasies which can be so frustrating for the would-be architects of the global economic order.

The third feature is, for me, the undeniable and inescapable conditionality of the myriad points of view that are heard in all debates, including the insights which faiths bring to the debate about the global economy and seek to incorporate in policy and practice. By 'conditionality' I mean that under different conditions different things would be said. Among these variable conditions are our personalities as individuals and groups, our historical development and current circumstances, our social status, our age and gender and our religious upbringing. Two of them stand out. One is the knowledge we happen to possess. It is limited or partial. If we knew more or we knew something else we would think differently. If we knew it all, our views would probably change altogether. The other is what we perceive to be our self-interest. It may lead us to preserve the status quo, adjust it, challenge it or change it, and in each case adorn our actions with moral and religious justifications.

Let me make four comments on this third feature of plurality before I move on. First, although it highlights the differences between us, it does not remove our commonality understood in a certain way. Ronald Preston certainly understood the point about conditionality including the role of self-interest in shaping our opinions. He recognized the need to ask who was advancing a particular point of view and why. He practised the hermeneutics of suspicion. Where he was open to criticism was in overestimating our shared human experience as a basis for reaching agreement: that in the end the destitute Ethiopian farmer and the Muslim rice grower in Bangladesh were more or less like middle-class Western academics and would see the point!

But if Preston is accused of overestimating what we have in common, there are countless examples of people of faith and no faith who insist it should not be underestimated. Here are three recent ones of mine. An Orthodox archbishop and theologian insisted to me in conversation that we can often agree on common values where we differ over dogma. It was an interesting rebuke to those who over-identify ethics with stories or narratives or different world views and so drive our moralities apart. It was also an interesting rerun of the old ecumenical tag that 'doctrine divides but service unites'. Again, a Peruvian economist has written recently about the common ground between Gutierrez, the liberation theologian, and Amartya Sen, the avowedly secular or a-religious developmentalist.[6] The Satsung Foundation in India has just published a book on the *Essential Unity of All Religions*. There are no surprises here and these sorts of examples, as we know, can be multiplied.

My own understanding of commonality is what Preston might have called a 'thin' one. It does not assume a wealth of shared experience though it does not need to deny it: 'If you prick me, do I not bleed?' It does not rest heavily on normative definitions of human nature such as their rationality or moral capacity, they themselves being subject to conditionality. For me it is the simple assumption, based on experience, that it is worth talking to other people; and here I have in mind talking to villagers and community leaders in India and Rwanda and to the congregation of the central mosque in Birmingham. We are unlikely to completely understand or always reach common ground. Commonality, however, means acting as if it makes sense to talk.

Second, if we recognize conditionality and that it cannot be avoided, since even the agreements which may to some extent rise above it are themselves conditioned, the choice between realism and prescriptivism in ethics, between whether moral values are part of some real, objective world out there waiting to be described or are made up and imposed on it by human beings, seems somewhat unreal. Even if there are objective, given, moral values structured into the nature of things, our grasp of them can only be conditioned and, where we absolutize them, it can only be fideistic. They are not absolutes. We only believe them to be absolute and for our own conditioned reasons. Claims to 'revelation' and to 'authority' do not represent privileged or immediate access to unconditioned truth. I mention this only to confess how strongly I perceive the world to be plural.

Third, conditionality is the close bosom friend of relativism. I am happy to use the word in one sense but not in another. The

---

[6] Javier M. Iguiniz Echeverria, 'Freedom in Sen and Gutierrez: Religious and Secular Common Ground' (unpublished paper).

views we bring to debates about the economic order, including those inspired by our religions faiths, are related to and affected by all the factors we have mentioned. Take the Christian teaching on usury, for example, which Ronald Preston expounded more than once and which has surfaced again in the Jubilee Debt Campaign, and the ways in which it has changed almost out of recognition under the weight of historical circumstances and the pressure of opportunism. Some degree of so-called 'flexibility' can also be discerned in Islamic teaching on loans and interest rates. But to acknowledge relativism in this sense is not to fall into relativism in another sense and regard moral debate as a free-for-all where anything goes and everything is equally justifiable and moral seriousness is dismissed with the cynical observation that 'it's all relative'. We can be serious in our search for the good and put our thinking to the test while acknowledging that those who do the searching are always subject to conditionality.

Fourth, 'conditionality' and 'relativism' are too often cast in only a negative light. They only make difficulties for us: they warn us how difficult it is to get at the truth; they point up the distances between human beings; they encourage us to distrust what other people have to say and to focus on the motive for saying it rather than the substance of what is said; and so on. Without denying these realities, 'conditionality' and 'relativism' should also be seen in a much more positive light. They could be renamed: 'complementarity'. They point us not just to limitations but to sources of enrichment. All of us are inescapably conditioned, but fortunately we are conditioned in different ways. Our knowledge and vantage points are partial, but fortunately they are partial in different ways. Encounters between conditioned people can therefore become corrective and complementary so that the end result is a richer harvest of human understanding and insight than if any of us stay within our own limitations and attempt to universalize our moral prescriptions from there. Our conditionality has a great deal of potential for our good.

Radical participation and the common good

Having looked at three features of plurality – the diversity of faiths, the untidiness of life on the ground, and our inescapable conditionality – we must now ask how best to respond to it. In stating my own preference I am not all that interested in completely dismissing those of others. In the spirit of what we have just said they can be complementary and not merely contradictory. One obvious example is Hans Kung's search for a 'Global Ethic'[7] which runs through all or most of the main religious traditions and which can provide us with a strong moral base for, among other things, global economic policies and practice. There is no room to do it justice here beyond saying on the positive side that it can help to mark out common ground and build confidence as a basis for co-operation: Kung refers to it as a declaration of peace between the world's religions. A global ethic can also provide strong ethical criteria against which to measure emerging and established policies. Human rights, not dissimilar to a global ethic, can function in the same way. So can the six fundamental principles of Catholic social teaching, including: Solidarity, Subsidiarity and the Preferential Option for the Poor. It should also be said that Kung's approach is more nuanced and aware of the issues raised by plurality than his critics sometimes suggest. On the more negative side a global ethic can sound like generalizations which are not a great deal of help when it comes to policy-making (where, for example, we are not arguing about whether or not to love our neighbour but what might turn out to be a loving economic policy that actually did our neighbour some good; and we are not debating the merits of distributive justice but how to distribute the wealth we create). It can also lose sight of the distinctive bite of a faith tradition.

My own preferred response to plurality is to promote 'radical participation' in policy-making and practice.[8] It moves beyond the debate which Preston and others pursued at one time with the World Council of Churches[9] where rational Western expertise could seem to be on one side and the popular opinions of poor and marginalized people on the other. Radical or thoroughgoing participation is a 'both–and' not an 'either–or' strategy. When it comes to incorporating the insights of religious faith into

[7] Hans Kung, *A Global Ethic for Global Politics and Economics* (Oxford: Oxford University Press, 1998).

[8] See Michael Taylor, *Not Angels but Agencies*, (London: SCM Press, 1995), pp. 165–68 and ibid. *Poverty and Christianity* (London: SCM Press, 2000), pp. 74–83.

[9] See *The Future of Ecumenical Social Thought: Report of an informal discussion of church leaders, theologians, social ethicists and laity, Berlin, May 29–June 3, 1992* (printed privately).

economic policy and practice, that will mean all faiths and all the diversity of views within them. Thoroughgoing participation will retain the respect for autonomous disciplines shown by Preston but be equally open to the insights, not of 'amateurs' and 'lay people' as against 'experts', but of people with different kinds of expertise culled from their day-to-day experience on the ground and in the field (I have heard them referred to as 'experts from poor communities'). Thoroughgoing participation will also take care to embrace the different social strata, men and women, young and old, the different estates or sectors of society, together with the so-called 'big picture' as seen by governments and the 'snapshots' taken by local groups and communities.

Obviously this kind of participation in policy-making is extremely difficult to manage and impossible to achieve. For one thing it has no logical boundaries. But we can err on the side of it. We can act, as Philip Wogaman might have said, with a presumption in favour of inclusiveness, believing that only in this way can we maximize the wisdom we need and harvest the wisdom that is available.[10]

To turn from the abstract to the particular, the Jubilee Campaign to cancel the debts of the poorest countries, which Preston criticized for mistakenly transferring an old biblical concept into a modern and alien environment, constantly ran up against the debate about another kind of 'conditionality'. On what conditions should these debts be cancelled, since it is no good freeing up money that was being spent on debt repayments to build schools and hospitals if it goes instead into the pockets of corrupt government officials or to buy arms to fight wars? The answer was that each country should draw up and publish a Poverty Reduction Strategy setting out its plans in detail, right down to which schools and hospitals would be built where and in what order of priority. Without such a Strategy (referred to in the jargon as a PRSP: Poverty Reduction Strategy Paper) no debts would be cancelled and no further concessional loans be made available. There was, however, a second equally important 'condition' and that was that the PRSPs should be drawn up by way of a more participatory process. One of the criticisms of the loans to poor countries which gave rise to the debt crisis in the

[10] See J. Philip Wogaman, *A Christian Method of Moral Judgment* (London: SCM Press, 1976).

first place was that they were largely the result of private, not to say covert, bilateral deals between the government of a poor country and donors like the World Bank and its G8 backers. The general population had no say in them. It did not know what had been agreed, let alone endorse it; but when things went badly wrong, it suffered the consequences. The PRSP process is now required to bring those people in. The result in many countries has been an interesting approximation to the thoroughgoing or 'radical participation' preferred as the proper response to plurality. The most frequent criticism of it has come where the process has not been participatory enough.

PRSPs include governments with their 'big pictures'. They include expert economists, civil servants, agriculturalists, and so forth. They have been criticized for not including sufficiently the private sector, a curious state of affairs since the privatization of services and the role of the private sector is much talked about and looked on with considerable favour by some and disfavour by others. The World Bank and the IMF insist that they are not involved in these participatory proceedings and that the result is the strategy of the government – of Uganda, for example, or Malawi – not of the Bank. That is clearly misleading, since if the strategy does not take account of the macroeconomic policies pursued by the Bank and the IMF it is unlikely to find favour or funding.

The most significant step towards wider participation, however, has been the inclusion of civil society. In most poor countries that has meant the NGO (non-governmental organization) commu- nity, some members of which are indigenous but many of which are linked to international organizations such as the OXFAMs of this world and the United Nations. Added to this are the 'faith communities'. In theory they should be distinguished from faith- based NGOs, like Christian Aid or Islamic Relief, though in practice they are not so easily separated. Sometimes faith communities distance themselves from civil society in an effort to maintain their own identity and not be seen as NGOs. Nevertheless, they are, or can be, part of the participatory process. Churches and mosques, for example, with their long history of providing education and healthcare, and with their presence in almost every local community, have much to contribute and can have a seat at the table along with everybody else. Here, then, is a significant step towards radical participation and, for me, there is a presumption in its favour. In principle we should support it as an appropriate response to plurality.

The consensus which emerges from a process like this – for example, in the case of the PRSP process it will be a strategy for poverty reduction and human development in a particular country and tied into its budget – is the only understanding of the 'Common Good'[11] that I can make much sense of, beyond the intention to seek the good of everyone.

If there is an objective, existing common good, we cannot know it objectively. It is not a fundamental a priori moral agreement underlying all our differences. It is not derived or deduced from a common understanding of human nature. It is more pragmatic than principled. It cannot assume a commonality of interest or shared context; rather, it looks for it. It is not a single good but the satisfaction of different goods or a 'plurality of ends'.[12] It is not decided by some, in Kantian style, as 'good' because they are prepared to universalize it rather patronizingly as good for everyone. It is not a global good by universal application but only in so far as it commands universal agreement. The common good is an ad hoc, limited agreement reached on particular matters in a particular context: in this case an economic and social strategy for a poor country where those involved, taking account of their different insights and interests, agree on what seems good for all of them for the time being. They may agree for different reasons. They may arrive at agreement by different routes. They nevertheless come to recognize common ground on which everyone has a better chance to flourish. The common good is not what some, however wise, well-meaning and morally impressive, say is the common good or is the good for somebody else whether rich or poor. The common good is what all involved agree is *their* common good.[13]

---

[11] Another subject of debate featured in Preston's writings; see Elford and Markham (eds.), *The Middle Way*, pp. 207–71.

[12] See Elford and Markham (eds.), *The Middle Way*, p. 204.

[13] See Normunds Kamergrauzis, *The Persistence of Christian Realism* (Uppsala: Uppsala University Press, 2001), pp. 211–12.

Principled, distinctive and valid

Having voted in favour of 'radical participation' and striving for consensus on the common good of those involved, a number of comments and qualifications need to be made. One should certainly be about the immense challenge to those who believe in it to learn better how to manage it so that it becomes equitable as a process, productive and decisive; but I leave all that, important as it is, on one side. I have four comments to make.

First, I described the outcome of a radically participatory process searching for consensus as 'more pragmatic than principled'. The outcome is a practical course of action, like a Poverty Reduction Strategy or a fair trade agreement, about which all come to agree but not necessarily (though the possibility should not be excluded) for the same principled reasons. So-called fair trade may be attractive to one party as an expression of justice but to another as being good for public relations and therefore good for business and wealth creation. If the outcome is pragmatic in that sense, it is not, however, unprincipled. The fact that it has become a common good only because in practice all have agreed to it does not rule out the possibility that all may have agreed to it for principled, though different, reasons. The participants in the search may not justify the outcome on the same moral or faith grounds but that does not mean that they have not in their different ways approached the search and adopted the outcome with a high degree of moral seriousness. An unavoidable plurality of moral and theological principles does not mean that people do not have any, or that they jettison them in reaching a consensus. It is conceivable that they might even improve on them.

My second comment could be regarded as a different version of the first. Some approaches to social ethics or social theology and their attempts to incorporate faith into social and economic policies have been criticized for losing sight of the distinctiveness of their faith traditions in favour of what everyone appears to have in common. The risk would seem particularly high when it comes to the kind of pragmatic, ad hoc consensus-seeking under discussion. The criticism might be levelled at an approach like that of global ethics where a host of religious insights seem to be levelled out into a collection of golden rules which few can be against. The same might be said for all methodologies which distil general principles out of particular stories, texts and doctrines and lose all their interesting but unmanageable idiosyncrasies in the process. The appeal to reason or common sense or shared human experience could be another example.

This tendency to lose sight of the distinctiveness of Christianity and therefore to sell it short, and presumably any social policy put forward in its name, is another of the criticisms levelled at Ronald Preston.[14] One example cited is the way he talks about justice in terms of fairness and distribution whereas in the biblical tradition justice has to do with solidarity with the poor and the constant struggle against all forms of oppression. In the Bible it has more of a 'liberating' than a 'liberal' flavour.[15]

The argument that the distinctiveness of Christianity should not be lost is perhaps seen at its most extreme in the writings of what I believe are called the New Orthodox. They seem to echo some of Barth's sayings of old with his over-direct moves from dogma to social policy. They not only insist that social teaching be firmly rooted in distinctive doctrinal teaching but come close to suggesting that where the outcome is not distinctive it is not Christian.

For me, the 'common good' cannot by definition be 'distinctive' in relation to any one religious faith. Indeed, it should not be so. There are several reasons for this. One is that in a plural world, as we are seeing, if one religion is too prominent in the public realm, and policies are over-identified with its teachings, it leads to perceptions of dominance and so to conflict. Secularism and the privatization of religion are often rightly condemned for abandoning the public for the private; but they may have had something to commend them as attempts to avoid religion playing an unhelpful role by being over-prominent or visible in public life. A second reason why the 'common good' cannot be distinctive in relation to any one religion arises from its own conditionality.

---

[14] For example, by Kamergrauzis in *The Persistence of Christian Realism*.

[15] It is interesting to note in passing that some unlikely modern institutions could now argue that they have been converted to the most radical and distinctive forms of Christianity by putting the poor first in their policies. The World Bank now describes itself as 'poverty focused'. The UN has signed up to the Millennium Development Goals which make it a priority to reduce poverty by at least half by 2015. The UK government's Department for International Development would claim to have radicalized the present government in terms of pro-poor policies, from levels of aid in the budget to debt cancellation. It could be argued that there is a welcome, distinctively Christian flavour about all of this!

Recognizing its own limitations, which of course many religions and their adherents do not, a religious tradition will be open to correction and completion by others in the participatory process and the search for common ground. Of course, that does not rule out the possibility that distinctive features of one faith tradition may come to be appreciated and therefore adopted by all.

Just as a pragmatic consensus is not an unprincipled consensus, so consensus which does not necessarily hold fast to or 'parade' the distinctive character of a religious tradition should not be regarded as a bad compromise, in the sense that that tradition has reneged on or ignored what it believes. It need not sell its soul and it should certainly draw quite firmly and doggedly on its own distinctive insights, such as the priority of the poor as a key feature of God's justice or righteousness, as it argues its way through. Indeed, this distinctiveness or difference is a major part of what a religious tradition has to bring to the dialogue. It can be seen negatively as its partiality but also, as we have said, more positively as its potential to awaken interest and enrich the process. One great lesson of interfaith dialogue is not to play down difference but to play it up, provided there is mutual respect for difference and the arguments believers build on it are transparent.

To come to a third comment, some will object that the outcome of the kind of participatory process I have opted for could be something far worse than an unprincipled, morally bland, pragmatic consensus. It could simply be wrong. Not a common good; not even a lowest common denominator; but a common bad. We are left with a general agreement which is dangerously mistaken (as some would say, of course, of the current global economic order: triumphant and without an alternative but profoundly wrong). So how is consensus on this common good to be validated?

If the question looks for an answer in terms of an independent, authoritative court of appeal, we know that an essentially plural and conditioned human community cannot have it. The only validation available to us is the agreement of those involved who give their consent to the outcome for their own good reasons. That is my understanding of the common good: good which those involved come to agree they have in common; the good that they judge will do them all good. That is not, however, the end of the story. For one thing, dissent will come eventually from within, as further experience and reflection reveal the holes in an agreed policy and practice; or dissent will come from without, as those not party to the consensus will raise their own voices. Added to this, growing maturity will accept that all common goods are to some extent provisional and will marry the necessary decisiveness and commitment, in relation to a Poverty Reduction Strategy in a poor country, for example, to a proper modesty and scepticism. Dissenting voices from within and without will therefore be given a hearing, and wrong-headedness will be exposed to critical and corrective voices. Dissenting voices, however, cannot simply overrule consensus but must win their points in an ongoing and widening participatory process that eventually arrives at a better one.[16]

Middle axioms

My fourth comment has to do with 'middle axioms': a methodological device in Christian social theology for doing exactly what we are talking about – getting faith into the social and economic orders. It dates back to earlier, headier days of ecumenical social ethics. It was a prominent feature of Ronald Preston's work. I was brought up on the concept myself.

I have thought about middle axioms as a practitioner in aid and development, and in particular contexts where getting faith into policies is never easy and the need for it not often appreciated. Drawing up Poverty Reduction Strategies is one of them. The World Bank's WDR 2004: *Making Services Work for Poor People*, is another. The services referred to are: healthcare, primary education, water and sanitation. They are closely related to the Millennium Development Goals for 2015 which include cutting the worst of poverty in half. The aim of the WDR 2004 is to highlight and promote policies and practices which actually work. The process of writing it is at least consultative and at best participatory, though some would say that, when it speaks of the poor as 'clients' and of making services work *for* them rather than of working *with* them, it is not participatory enough. I myself am involved with a modest attempt to put together a contribution to it

---

[16] Failure to reach consensus raises a series of questions including that of a moral obligation to compromise.

from the perspectives of the world's faith communities.[17] It is a specific attempt to put faith into an important aspect of the global economic order and to be part of an inclusive effort to find consensus and promote the common good, that is, policies and practices which all the parties involved (including the not-so poor) agree will benefit them and bring them the education they want for their children, the healthcare they need for young and old alike, and the water and sanitation which will be the cause of good health instead of multiplying disease. The debate leading to the final report is based on successive drafts then made public by the World Bank.

Clearly this discussion draws heavily on what Preston and others would have referred to as the autonomous disciplines with their expertise: for example, in economics, engineering, social science and development. Islamic scholars refer to them as 'scientific disciplines'. It is also drawing on local knowledge and experience which insists that, because of history, geography and culture, what might work in one place will not necessarily work in another. One size does not fit all. Plurality cannot be ignored.

In addition there are the ideological or theological debates which can provoke faith communities into speaking about their faiths and values. One such debate, which will surprise no one, focuses on the issue of the privatization of services like education, healthcare, water and sanitation. The World Bank and the authors of the draft WDR 2004 are already suspected of an ideological bias in favour of privatization and against the state, which reflects their commitment to, not to say quasi-religious belief in, the free market as the source of human good. To be fair, the later drafts were not obviously biased in that way. They seemed more ready to say: that privatization works better in some circumstances than in others; that there are no universal answers; that careful distinctions need to be made between responsibility for the provision of services and the actual means of delivering them. Nevertheless, there is the strong flavour of theological debate in the contributions from faith communities who can sometimes map out fairly direct routes from privatization through the market place to what they see as denials of God's ownership of, say, water and the right of every human being to have access to it and their fundamental calling to share and co-operate with each other rather than to

---

[17] Organised by the World Faiths Development Dialogue.

compete. We are dealing with resources, not commodities; for sharing, not for profit.

The attempt to find consensus on *Making Services Work for Poor People'* involves, therefore, the exact heady mix of theological or ideological insights, the expertise of autonomous disciplines and the data from empirical observation and experience with which Preston was so familiar. I, nevertheless, find most aspects of the debate about middle axioms, to which he contributed right to the end of his life, curiously tangential to what we might call 'radical participation seeking consensus' as a methodological response to plurality; and I say that with these two practical examples in mind: the participatory processes leading to Poverty Reduction Strategies and to the WDR 2004.

To be more specific, what seems tangential or even irrelevant is the deliberate attempt to arrive at middle axioms or, if we are to avoid the term, 'general directives in less than general situations' (such as 'globalization' or an HIPC country) as a stage (if not a strictly logical step) in getting faith into policies or relating faith to social and economic issues. I am wondering why.

As far as I can tell, besides wanting to find a plausible way of involving faith in public policy-making, there are four things which Preston particularly sought to uphold in adopting the middle axiom approach.[18]

1. One was to be clear about the proper limits to the Church's competence. It is competent to expound its own teaching and it is competent to go half way in spelling out the broad implications of that teaching in particular situations. It is not competent to make detailed proposals. The reasons given are: the detailed proposals are too uncertain with so many factors involved; they are the responsibility of lay people; and, if the Church does put them forward as Church, they are in danger of being over-identified with the Gospel that always transcends them. There is no denying that Christians need to go all the way and make detailed proposals, but the Church as Church should not.

There is a kind of protectiveness here that seems unreal, certainly in the arenas I have in mind. Two comments occur to me. First, whether the Church is competent or not, does it not

---

[18] See Ronald H. Preston, *Church and Society in the Late Twentieth Century* (London: SCM Press, 1983), pp. 141–56 and Elford and Markham (eds.), *The Middle Way*, pp. 267–69.

have an obligation to go beyond the middle ground to more detailed commitments? The individual Christian certainly does. Why not the Church in solidarity, shall we say, with its members and with society, especially where they are extremely poor? Second, if competence is the issue then it is not a matter of whether the Church has it but a matter of which competence it is exercising: competence, for example, to expound its own teaching or, on another occasion, competence to draw on the wisdom available to it to make proposals for public policy. There can be competence in each case, and in each case it will come with the vulnerability born of the conditional nature of its doctrine, its ethical principles and its detailed proposals, calling all along for commitment but also for scepticism. Even Preston seems to accept that the difference between the middle ground and the detailed proposal is a difference of degree rather than of kind. (I will resist a third comment here which might have wondered what we mean by 'the Church'. Is it, for example, Rowan Williams when he approves of detention centres for asylum seekers?)

2. In promoting middle axioms, Preston also wanted to reduce disagreements among Christians and so strengthen the unity of the Church. If that was a political tactic, which I doubt, I understand it. We cannot, of course, be against agreement. If we are to act together for the common good we must work for consensus. But radical participation will not seek consensus at this particular middle point but at the point of specific agreements on policies to reduce poverty and make services work for poor people. Indeed, as we have said, the parties to those agreements may arrive at them by different routes and for different reasons, including different mediating principles or middle axioms.

3. In promoting middle axioms Preston also sought to uphold a certain pastoral concern to offer wisdom and guidance to individual Christians on the general direction in which they should be going. The example he used more than once, from another generation, is that Christians should generally work for full employment (as against leaving job levels to market forces) though the Church cannot give much guidance as to how exactly this is to be achieved. In the settings I have in mind it is not clear that directives of this sort would add much useful guidance to the more general principles of, say, Catholic Social Teaching, so confidently deployed in a recent Catholic response (unpublished) to the draft of WDR 2004 and its proposals on water supplies. And

before middle axioms can guide they have to be painstakingly worked out.

4. The only added value I can think of is that middle axioms come blessed with Preston's fourth and final concern in promoting them, and that is that they come with a degree of authority. They are more than just another opinion. They shift the burden of proof onto those who disagree with them. If you ask, however, about the source of this authority there are certainly hints that it lies in the close relation between middle axioms and the doctrinal and ethical teachings of the Church, but there are more definite indications that it stems from the fact that middle axioms are less relative and, as he says, 'more probable'. Yet this is exactly the authority that radical participation tries to establish, but not at some middle level. By allowing partial perceptions, conditioned in all sorts of ways, to complement and criticize and correct each other, the consensus reached on particular, detailed strategies and policies for poverty reduction are themselves 'less relative' and therefore more 'authoritative' and 'probable' and entitled to our confidence.

Radical participation seeking consensus as a response to pluralism implies for me, therefore, a less structured methodology than the middle axiom approach. It is serious about its moral principles and its religious beliefs but it does not think first about establishing general directives and then moving through them to particular conclusions, and it is not concerned about the status and competence of official religious institutions. The goal is consensus as to what should be done and how, and as faith communities take part in arriving at it they will contribute their special insights and what illumination they can to the debate at whatever level and at every turn. They will win their way only by the perceived merit of their argument.

My hesitations about middle axioms do not exclude the possibility that consensus takes the form of a 'rule of thumb'; for example, in handling privatization, that the more basic the need being met (like water), the greater the bias against the purer forms of private provision: a rule of thumb which arises out of Christianity and other faiths, and from empirical observation.

Counterbalancing power

A final concern arises from at least two considerations. One is the fear that we can sometimes make too much of a meal of getting faith into the economic order by thinking more highly of our methodological debates than we ought to think. I say this probably after a good going over by colleagues in highly intelligent, highly committed Christian circles (such as Christian Aid) who are willing to go so far with theology but not much further. They are all for taking care of the weak and the vulnerable; they are all for reasonable opportunities for all to make a living; they are all for respecting the poorest as having a contribution to make and a right to make it; they are all for holistic understandings of human development; they are all for taking care of the created order; they are all for subsidiarity and other similar principles. They can connect much of this with a righteous God who creates us to live not for bread alone, to reflect God's image and to share the resources of God's world. And they can shape and test policies according to these and similar principles. By doing so they put their faith into their campaigning and into their policy-making and practice in aid and development. A good half of me will go along with that. The other half will test the arguments about methodology which I have been happily pursuing and the time and energy we spend on them by asking whether or not they open up ways to more fruitful policies and practices for the sake of the poorest. I believe that radical participation carries no guarantee, but probably does.

But my final concern arises from a second consideration as well. 'Radical participation seeking consensus' is crucially important because we need all the wisdom and insights we can get from all quarters if poverty is to be reduced and many more human beings are to have a chance to flourish. It assumes, however, a great deal of goodwill. It assumes that very different people actually want to get together and, by way of often long and difficult encounters, seek each other's good and not just their own. This massive assumption should not be discounted (as Ronald Preston recognized when he upheld the doctrine of original righteousness) but neither can it ignore one factor that may be more significant than anything else in shaping the plurality of views round the negotiating table, and that is the various interests of the parties involved, together with their tendency to promote and protect those interests, and their ability or inability to do so because of their power in the situation or lack of it.

In the present debates about the privatization of services, including the supply of water, it is a very real fear that such strategies are advanced mainly because they serve the interests not of ideologues but of large companies eager to see service provision included in the General Agreement on Tariffs and Trade and so excluded from present constraints on market forces. Any hopes we may put on radical participation as an appropriate response to plurality, including the plurality of faiths, may come to nothing if we do not take account of the only real difference between rich and poor besides the disparity of their resources. The difference is not one of virtue, or morality, or intelligence, or dependence, or diligence, or self-interest. It is the huge disparity of opportunity to pursue and protect self-interest. In other words, there is a huge disparity of power.

Power must be balanced and counterbalanced for negative and positive reasons: negatively to prevent the more powerful in every community, whether global, national or local, from putting the weak at a disadvantage; positively to put everyone in a position to make their contribution and further their cause; in other words, to be included not in gesture consultations but in radically participative processes which at the moment, for example, the World Trade Organization and some PRSP processes like that in Albania, are not, and of which all talk of partnership with the South by Northern governments and NGOs is a caricature for as long as they remain locked together in an 'ideology of superiority'.

To its credit, the draft Overview, WDR 2004, recognizes that 'power' is an issue. It has some nice if somewhat hackneyed illustrations of what can be done at the local level. If education services in remote areas of poor countries are to work for poor people, for example, then parents and families might be given a central role in hiring and firing the school teachers and in regularly monitoring their work and attendance. In this and other such ways the report speaks of the need for 'restoring people's power in service delivery' (para 15) and in client-provider relationships. Elsewhere it recognizes the need 'to strengthen poor people's ability to influence policy-makers' through advisory groups and coalitions as well as the electoral process (paras 28 and 29). In general the report concludes that many of the changes

needed to make services work for poor people 'involve fundamental shifts in power' (para 69).

Since we are talking about incorporating the insights of faith
into social and economic policy and practice, we should note that
the principle of counterbalancing power, long upheld in the
traditions of Christian social theology, is of course deeply rooted
in Christian belief and its realistic analysis of human nature, which
recognizes our potential to be both creative and destructive given
the opportunity. It is a principle that must accompany all attempts
at policy-making if they are not to come to grief. It raises a whole
host of issues, most of them familiar but often sadly neglected by
sentimental believers and do-gooders. We can but mention some
of them here. They include issues within the participatory
processes themselves, like access to information and the use of
language. They include devices for giving power to poor people
like the one just quoted but also, for example, decentralized
government and the more local, internalized economies which
offer not independence from global economic forces but some
ability to moderate and resist their effects. They include strategies
which recognize that those who have power rarely cede power and
that it has to be taken in various ways by those who have little or
no power. They include democratic instruments of global
governance and institutions of international law based on
human rights, by which the powerful are held to account. They
include looking at arguments about the merits of co-operation
and competition in the economic order as arguments about
power as well as about the nature and destiny of human beings.
Finally, though not exhaustively, they include educating self-
interest. Power will be exercised according to the perceived
interest of the powerful. They will not easily cede that power. They
may act differently if they understand their self-interest in a
different light and come to believe, for example, that in a
terrifying, conflictual, environmentally damaged world, their self-
interest lies in more distributive and sustainable economic and
social policies.

Conclusion

In conclusion, let me return to the ambiguity of my title: Faith in
the Global Economic System. It reflects our concern, and Ronald

Preston's concern, that faith insights should be incorporated into the substance of our economic policies. Hence the discussion about methodology. But it also raises the question as to whether we have much faith or confidence in the global economic system and its ability in particular to deliver a better life for the poor of the earth. On that issue opinion remains deeply divided. For my part, confidence will grow in so far as two discrete but interrelated strategies are pursued at the same time. The first I have called: 'radical participation seeking consensus'. The second is the constant effort at many levels to balance and counterbalance power. Without the one we shall not draw out the wisdom we require. Without the other, before we even seek that wisdom, we shall demonstrate that we are not wise.

7

King Mohosoth and Princess Amara[1]

An exercise in 'radical participation' with implications for Christian social action

I regard Ted Wickham's work on *Church and People in an Industrial City*[2] as a fine example of the critical reflection on our Christian practice which is always required of us but which we are not often brave or obedient enough to do. He reflected on the failure of the Church, as typified by the churches of Sheffield, to embrace the working classes, and put forward theological and structural proposals to put it right. Many of Wickham's proposals were never realized or have faded away, along perhaps with Britain's manufacturing base, and the Church's alienation from the working classes has not been reversed but become more widespread among all classes, as church attendance continues to decline. But if critical reflection on our seeming failure is needed here, it is also needed in other areas of the Church's mission, including the one which has occupied me in recent years: its mission to reduce poverty and enhance human development not least in the economically poorer countries of the world. Where poverty is still rife, the gap between the richest and the poorest tends to widen, a sense of injustice grows, children still die unnecessarily in their thousands, and conflict and terror are fuelled. Despite all the efforts of the modern world development movement, in which the churches have played an honourable

[1] The annual E. R. Wickham Lecture, given in Manchester Cathedral, UK in May 2004.

[2] E. R. Wickham, *Church and People in an Industrial City* (Cambridge: Lutterworth Press, 1957).

part, there is plenty of room for critical reflection so that greater wisdom can nourish practical obedience.

When it comes to being wise, Wickham insisted the Church could not be wise by simply drawing on its own resources. It had to learn from other disciplines, in his case those of historical research and sociology which he used so brilliantly to lay bare the truth that, if the working classes were outside the Church, their absence had nothing to do with their godliness or lack of it. That insistence on what we now call 'interdisciplinary work' and respect for 'the autonomy of disciplines' has been enshrined in the tradition of Christian social ethics in which I was nurtured, chiefly by Ronald Preston, and nothing that I have to say is intended to undermine it.

Our world, however, in contrast to Wickham's who, under-standably, never mentions ethnicity or multiculturalism or other faiths, is characterized for me by words he would not have used in the way I do, and they are: 'pluralism' and 'relativism'. They call, not for a weakening of his emphasis on the need to learn from others if we are to be wise, but a strengthening and broadening out of it both because we are more aware of how rich and varied and attainable those resources are, and because we are aware of the partial nature of them all, including our own. The variety of resources available to us includes experts and specialists in economics, sociology, developmental studies or whatever, but also lay practitioners on the ground; it includes men and women, poor and rich, local and global perspectives and, especially now for me, the insights of different faith traditions, all of them with varied histories, experiences, cultures and vested interests colour-ing their perspectives as they do ours. The more these resources are brought together in what I call 'radical participation' (radical meaning 'thoroughgoing') and partial insights are allowed to critique, correct and complement one another, the more oppor-tunities there are for the body of wisdom to grow, as long as we remember that it can never be complete, or beyond question, however impressive the consensus may be; and that it can never be a substitute at the end of the day for making up our own minds and taking responsibility for our own decisions. 'Radical partici-pation' is not an automatic route to problem solving but it is a promising and indeed essential way to greatly improve the quality of reflective knowledge and experience with which we can address our problems and failures.

Since I have argued this elsewhere[3] I will not argue it again at length. What follows instead is an extremely modest exercise in trying to put radical participation into practice. The focus of attention, as I have indicated, is poverty reduction and human development: what we mean by them and how we achieve them in the light of some progress but far from overwhelming success and what some see as a global situation all too likely to go into reverse. The actual participatory encounter was between 11 faith communities each of which had provided a case study about their involvement in these issues.[4] In the background, but making its presence felt like the spectre at what turned out to be quite a feast, was what I shall call 'mainstream' or 'Western' development as represented by international financial institutions (IFIs) like the IMF and the World Bank; the G8 and their government departments like DFLD in the UK; many Western NGOs including the Christian Aids of this world; and, let it be said, my own attitudes and assumptions. The encounter took place in New Delhi in February 2004, when representatives of these communities spent three days together. The limits of the exercise are obvious. The case studies are few and to some extent arbitrarily selected. They were, however, carefully prepared, revised and edited with considerable rigour and led to a discussion about poverty and development which for once was not dominated by the North, or Christianity and its more secular offsprings. With such a narrow database, this can hardly claim to be quantitative research. It was, however, qualitative research in two ways. It produced a wide range of opinions and it involved a wide range of perspectives: experts and lay, women and men, local and regional, interdisciplinary, multicultural and interfaith. All present were deeply involved with poor communities. A number adopted simple lifestyles, though none would claim to be poor themselves. But whatever the quality or the size of it, what matters in the end is what we learn from such interesting encounters, and what we do with what we learn.

In the rest of this chapter I will begin by briefly introducing the participants and their case studies. I will then note, again briefly,

---

[3] See, for example, Chapters 3 and 6 above and Taylor, *Poverty and Christianity*, pp. 74–7.

[4] The case studies are available on the website of the World Faiths Development Dialogue <www.wfdd.org.uk>.

one or two areas of convergence between what they have to say and 'mainstream development' policies and practice before going on to discuss in more detail two areas in which the contrast between what they have to say and mainstream opinions, including my own, is striking and thought-provoking, and ask about the implications for Christian social action.

The case studies

The 11 case studies came from four religious traditions.

1. Three of the case studies were Hindu-inspired. The Swadhyaya Movement dates back to the 1930s and 40s. It draws on the classical wisdom of the Gita and Upanishads. It has about 200,000 volunteers in India, often business and professional people, who travel regularly to the villages to share their message in a direct and personal way. It is a spiritual message about inner-transformation and drawing close to God but through collective activities often of a developmental kind that seem far from 'spiritual' in the conventional sense. They include farming and fishing where the proceeds are used for the common good. Swadhyayans, in this and other ways, refuse to separate the inward from the outward, the individual from the social, the material from the spiritual. Collective fishing boats are called 'floating temples'.

The Swaminarayans were founded in the nineteenth century in Gujarat where there are still millions of followers. In many ways they are conservative Hindus, as reflected in their attitudes to women and to caste, but have been at the forefront of social reform and can sound surprisingly modern and secular. There is a strong ascetic emphasis in the austere lifestyle of the monks or swamis but it does not spill over into a dualistic or other-worldly point of view. Many of the lay followers are extremely wealthy but generous with their time and money. While their devotion takes a very practical form (water conservation was the main example quoted) they are well known for building temples of monumental proportions including those at Akshardham and, in the UK, in Neasden, North London.

Vivekananda Girijana Kalyana Kendra (VGKK) was founded in 1981 by a medical doctor – Dr Sudashan – living and working among the Soligas tribes in the thickly forested hills of Karnataka in south India. Sudashan was inspired to follow the Vedantic path of Karma Yoga, drawing close to God through practical work rather than mysticism. VGKK has a commitment to combining what is best in a traditional way of life with the benefits of modern education and science. As a result, nature worship, with its devotion to trees and birds, herbal medicines and local birth practices are all respected alongside modern medical facilities, as these remote people encounter the outside world.

2. Two case studies were Christian-inspired. The first, Tokombéré, was founded by a Catholic missionary, Simon Mpeke, among the Kirdi people of Cameroon. 'Kirdi' means 'unbelievers', but in Mpeke's opinion they already knew God. Running through fairly familiar programmes is a recurring emphasis on people as the necessary agents as well as the beneficiaries of their own development, an emphasis rooted in faith in their abilities and potential as made in the image of God.

Community AIDS Response (CARE), though formally a secular NGO, draws much of its inspiration from evangelical Christian faith. Founded in 2001, it is concerned as much for the carers as for the victims of HIV and AIDS. In 2003 some 15,000 people, mainly from the poorer urban areas and townships in and around Johannesburg, were assisted. It takes an explicitly holistic approach, combining spiritual, emotional and medical care.

3. Three case studies were Muslim-inspired. Nahdlatul Ulama (NU) from Indonesia is one of the largest Muslim organizations in the world. Its association for women, the subject of the case study, spreads across thousands of villages and involves millions of women. The focus of its work is on reproductive health and family welfare, increasing the control of women over their own bodies and in so doing, to use their words, 'to satisfy the inner self'. NU's approach is in contrast to more conservative Islamic teaching on the one hand, which rules out birth control altogether, and the aggressive policies of the Suharto regime in the 1960s on the other, which subordinated the rights and welfare of women to coercive programmes of population control for the sake of economic growth. Indonesia's birth rate did fall between 1971 and 1997 but only after organizations like NU, with their respect for the rights of women, became involved.

Asian Muslim Action Network (AMAN) links Muslim communities in many countries. It cited two particular communities in its case study. Both had evolved against a background of violence.

a. The first was Gono Unnayan Prochesta (GUP): People's Development Efforts founded in 1973 in Bangladesh following a bloody war of independence. GUP fosters a non-bureaucratic style of leadership and values people-centred development, empowerment and participation. Working in over 300 villages its activities range from income-generating projects to peace forums and village associations (somittes) which link people together in communities and foster solidarity. b. Cambodian Islamic Youth Association (CIYA) was founded in 1999, following Pol Pot and the Khmer Rouge, in an effort to recover the identity of the Muslim community but in ways which enhanced understanding and co-operation with others (almost all of them Buddhist) in social reconstruction.

The Addis Ababa Muslim Women's Council, the third Muslim-inspired case study, was founded in 1997 to encourage women to participate in social, economic and political development, emphasising both their rights and their responsibilities. A central concern has been to counteract the unfair treatment of women in the Sharia courts and oppose practices like female circumcision (clitoridectomy), all of which are defended as Islamic when in fact, it is argued, they are contrary to Islamic teaching and owe far more to traditional custom and practice.

4. The final three case studies were Buddhist-inspired. Sarvodaya Shramadana Movement (SSM) was founded in Sri Lanka in 1958 by a charismatic Buddhist. He organized work camps where students shared the life of poor villagers and worked alongside them on development projects such as building roads, digging wells, clearing irrigation canals and planting trees. In the period 1999 to 2000, three thousand volunteers worked in 11,400 villages. The camps in turn inspired the villagers themselves to work together for the common good, helped and supported by wider networks including national institutions providing specialized services. Buddhist monks play a leading role in SSM, which draws heavily on Buddhist teaching. Even its title includes Buddhist concepts: 'Sarvodaya' refers to the 'awakening' of the people and 'Shramadana' to the 'giving and volunteering' which enriches others and brings happiness to oneself.

Santi Sena (meaning a group of people who work for peace and social welfare), like the Cambodian Islamic Youth Association, was founded in the aftermath of conflict and genocide. It is situated on the Cambodian border with Vietnam. Every one of its activities is explicitly supported by Buddhist teaching, whether agriculture, gender awareness, conservation, education or conflict management. Santi Sena is led by monks but involves local people in decision-making and makes full use of their skills and resources.

Finally, Engaged Buddhism began in Thailand (Siam) in the 1930s in reaction to the perceived degradation of Buddhism and its monastic community (Sangha) under the influence of modernization. It has become increasingly critical of consumerism and advocates a simple way of life closer to nature and in community. In two respects it adopts a 'both–and' approach. While emphasizing the need for inner transformation and teaching the Eightfold Path, it takes seriously the need for social action and structural change – hence the title 'Engaged' Buddhists, engaged as they are with transforming the social order. Again, while upholding traditional values which have been eroded under Western influence, it appropriates the more positive elements of modernization. Activities include leadership training, training monks in community development, providing support and information to local communities and an ashram close to Bangkok inspired by Gandhi and combining spiritual practice with political action.

Here then are the participants in this exercise in 'radical participation': 11 case studies from four religious traditions in eight countries of the 'South' engaging with the mainstream, Western approach to development including, in many respects, my own. The case studies are by no means representative or even typical of the faith traditions which inspire them. Such traditions are varied in themselves and contain contrasting elements: more conservative (like Hindus who look more to the Smritis or codes of conduct than to the Shritis), less progressive, more pietistic, more influenced by the West. Some draw their inspiration from the same religious texts in order to perpetuate problems, like conflict and discrimination against women, that others are trying to overcome. All of which underlines the limited and non-quantitative nature of the exercise, even though some of the communities described have very large followings. Nevertheless, the case studies push us beyond the parameters within which we often do our thinking and so encourage us to deepen the quality of the critical reflection which arises from our dissatisfaction with past and present practice, and nourish our decisions about the future.

Convergence

There are a number of significant points of convergence between what the case studies have to say about poverty reduction and human development and what I have labelled the 'mainstream Western approach'. Many of the actual projects or programmes are familiar and might well have been funded by Western donors. Examples include education and literacy, healthcare, management of the natural environment including forestry and water conservation, irrigation schemes, agriculture, skills training, credit unions, income-generating projects, co-operatives and gender awareness training.

There is also a good deal of convergence, not just on what is done but on the way in which it is done. Much of contemporary 'development-speak' seems to be shared by everyone. Here are four examples.

The first is about 'participation'. Development is not something which is done for people, or even with people, by involving them in projects designed by someone else. Development is done by the people themselves out of a fundamental respect for them and their abilities. They are the agents of development as well as the beneficiaries. It is their needs which are to be met. They set the priorities and often they know best how their goals can be reached. Western agencies can be heard talking in these terms as well as these faith communities of the South.

A second example is about 'empowerment' and is closely related to the first. It can be fairly argued that the essential difference between rich and poor, apart from material wealth and the lack of it, is one of power. The rich have the wherewithal to pursue their self-interests to an extent which the poor have not. The road to justice is therefore the road of empowerment. That would certainly be one of my own fundamental convictions, to which I will return, and it is strongly reflected in the case studies. Two forms of empowerment are mentioned. One is personal. Individual men and women are empowered when they gain self-respect and confidence. It can be brought about by education, awareness training, encouragement and by simply being treated as people who are as capable of dealing with their lives as anyone else. The other form of empowerment has more of a political edge to it and emphasizes the importance of communities organizing themselves and standing together in solidarity with one another for purposes of mutual help but also in the face of external forces which all too easily ride roughshod over them. The empowerment of women in Indonesia became particularly important and decisive in the face of Suharto's programme of population control.

A third example of convergence is, again, closely related to the previous one, and that is the human rights approach to development. This has influenced the development debate in at least two ways in recent years. Development is often talked about in terms of goals and targets; indeed the 'Millennium Development Goals' (MDGs) are top of the global development agenda at the moment. Yet they too easily let development actors off the hook. The goals are desirable goals to be met if and when governments can meet them, and that is about the sum of their liabilities. A human rights approach, however, insists that education, healthcare and livelihoods are not desirable goals but essentials which everyone has a right to, here and now, and which governments and developers have a legal obligation to provide. They are not matters of generosity but of obligation. As a result, and this is the second way in which the debate has changed, communities of poor people should be organized and trained to stand up for themselves and demand from their governments what is theirs by right and what is a government's duty to provide. The case studies do not always use the term 'human rights' but they do talk about 'people's rights' and 'women's rights', drawn from the Qur'an for example, and so take a rights-based approach.

A fourth example concerns respect for traditional practices. All agree that long-established traditions are by no means beyond criticism. Quite the contrary, they can be extremely detrimental and oppressive, as in the case of female circumcision. But that is not to deny that they enshrine a great deal that is of enduring value, such as an understanding of a particular ecology and how to care for it, or traditional medicines, or birthing practices which in some communities have an astonishing rate of success in safe deliveries. Mainstream development, closely identified with modernization, may not be over enthusiastic about the value of older ways, but it has become more open to it as one aspect of people-centred development.

This exercise in 'radical participation', then, produces a strong sense of convergence at a number of significant points both on what is done and how it is done. To be fair, at times it may be more evident than real. If all are in favour of 'education', for example, the content, ethos and quality of education that is looked for may be very different. And, in two respects at least, some of the case study writers regard what I have called points of convergence as points of difference. They do not regard much of mainstream development as anything like 'people-centred'; and if the poor are to be given the opportunity to make their own futures in a sustainable way, the West is criticized for the way its agencies come and go with their funds and their changing policies. They fail to stand by communities over the long periods of time required, playing a supportive role and exercising patience.

Where there is convergence it may be interesting to speculate as to why it has occurred. Is it in itself an example of Westernization, or of the better side of 'globalization' where growing encounters allow for mutual influence and learning? Does it arise out of basic needs and instincts – even moral instincts – which many of us share, whatever our differences? Interesting though such speculation may be, it may not be as important or useful as mapping out and affirming this common ground, shared by many for whatever differing reasons, as a basis for co-operation in a plural world.

Contrast: spirituality

I turn to the next part of the discussion and the first of two striking areas, not of convergence, but of contrast.

The first, at first sight, seems to be an area of convergence! It has to do with broadening the concept of development to make it more *holistic*. This is now a word on everybody's lips in North and South, in the mainstream and in the case studies. Development is not just 'economic development'. It is about cultural and social development, and it must deal with people and their communities in the round.

But if everyone pays lip-service to this idea, the case studies tend to regard it as a point of difference, not of agreement, between them and the mainstream and on three grounds. First of all there is a strong feeling that the Western mainstream approach is not holistic at all but almost purely economic. The basic Western assumption is that economic growth is the key to poverty reduction and development. The measures to be taken are economic in character. The GNP (gross national product) of poor countries must rise. Liberalization must open them up to trade their way out of poverty. Investment must be encouraged by risk-free, good governance. Debts should be cancelled only if Poverty Reduction Strategies are in place and conform to the macro-economic policies of multilateral agencies and the G8. The levels of economic aid should be increased. The much-talked-of mechanism for making up-front funds available to achieve the MDGs is an International Finance Facility (IFF). Even if some of the MDGs have to do with healthcare, education and gender equality, the sine qua non for achieving them is economic growth, and the well-being of people and countries is seen to be grounded in a greater degree of material prosperity. It is all about money. Nobody, I would hope, questions the need to ensure that everyone has a decent, sustainable livelihood and that that requires us to take economic realities very seriously. The criticism is that economic development is relied on to produce the required results to the exclusion of almost everything else.

A second reason for disagreement over the issue of holism has to do with its 'integrity'. Some would say that even if the importance of social and cultural issues is acknowledged, they are then dealt with as discrete entities rather than as an interrelated whole. Economics may not be all that matters but it should be left to get on with its own business. To emphasize the opposite point of view, one of the case studies tends to talk of an 'integrated' rather than a 'holistic' approach to development.

A third disagreement about 'holism', however, is the most striking and the most important for our discussion. The case studies, unlike the mainstream, persistently add another dimension to a holistic profile of development: not just economic and social and cultural, but *spiritual* as well. The mainstream would wish to hide such a concern within references to culture, or to ignore it altogether.

The picture is somewhat different if we use the word 'religion' rather than 'spirituality'. The mainstream may not like religion all that much but it now accepts that religion plays an important part in development and that, however reluctantly, it has to deal with it. On the whole, mainstream economic development has seen religion in a negative light. It can be the focus of conflict and a source of conservatism. It complicates issues unnecessarily for those who see economics as an autonomous, technical discipline dealing with how things work in the market place. Politics, ideology and value judgments are not its business, whereas they are the oxygen of religion. Better not to get involved.

Now, however, mainstream development seems to have little choice. Too many issues post-9/11 are perceived to have both an economic and religious identity, whether it be growing conflict in Israel, Palestine and Iraq; oil supplies; security; or a growing sense of injustice. If they will never be resolved by military force, they might at least be eased by progress in development along the lines of the MDGs; which brings us to the instrumental reason for mainstream interest in religion. Religious organizations and communities already contribute hugely to health and education programmes across the world. They are present in every place and have huge potential as agents of community development and allies in the urgent fight against HIV/AIDS. If they can be co-opted as partners in development, rather than held at arms length as problematic, they can do much to strengthen the hand of mainstream development at the present time; hence the current talk by the World Bank and others of 'scaling-up' the development programmes of religious communities. The IFIs would prefer to co-operate on a pragmatic basis, avoiding too much ideological and principled debate, but co-operate they now realize they must.

The controversial point raised by the case studies is not, however, about religion as a partner in mainstream economic development. The point is about spirituality as part of a holistic vision of what a process of human development sets out to achieve. It aims to develop a sustainable economic basis for life. It aims to develop communities and what we now call their 'social capacity', where good social relations lead to benefits for all. It aims to respect and strengthen culture in all its diversity, though not uncritically and not without attention to social cohesion. But, according to the case studies, in contrast to Western mainstream development, a holistic vision aims to develop spirituality as well.

'Spirituality' is a very slippery word. There are many aspects to it, many of them referred to in the case studies, so we must try to be clear, not about a correct meaning for a word, but about what exactly is being said. Here are five examples of what is being said, either explicitly or implicitly in the case studies.

First, spirituality has to do with taking religious teaching and its implications seriously into account or, as more often happens, appealing to religious teachings in support of the actual substance of development policy and practice. It is rooted in religious faith. For Christians, for example, respect for people and their ability to be the creative agents of their own development is rooted in the teaching that we are made in the image of God. For Hindus, the appeal is to the Upanishads. For Muslim women, protesting against injustice in the Sharia courts and female mutilation, the Qur'an is cited, affirming, for example, that sexual relations between men and women are for purposes of reproduction but also for pleasure. The insistence on 'rights' again looks for support in the Qur'an and Hadith. Buddhists incorporate spiritual concepts like 'dana' into the names of their development organizations, and in one of the case studies all activities are systematically justified by quotations, in the manner of proof-texting.

Second, spirituality has to do not so much with the way religious teachings inform the substance of development policies and practice but the way it inspires, motivates and strengthens those who get involved. It does not only tell you what to do; it moves you to do it and, where things get difficult, offers you resources which enable you to persevere and not lose hope.

Third, and most at odds with the mainstream and with myself, spirituality is about inner transformation, whereby people involved in development are changed. The nature of the change is described in various ways and they are not mutually exclusive. It may be the adoption of new values and virtues such as unselfishness, love and humility. Some talk of purity of motive and the constant need to be mindful of what our motives are. Buddhists speak of a spiritual awakening (sarvodaya), maybe to the divine within us, leading to a growing sense of self-esteem and a renewed confidence which overcomes fear and a sense of powerlessness. Others speak about self-acceptance and inner peace and harmony.

Fourth, spirituality is not spoken of as a purely private matter unrelated to the public world of development practice. The inward and the outward are inextricably linked. One case study puts the reverse point quite strongly. If inward spiritual renewal is to come about it will be through practical activities, like working alongside one another to overcome poverty, which don't look particularly spiritual at all: 'As we build the road, the roads builds us.' But whichever way round, inner and outer cannot be separated and either succeed or fail together. Love for God is married to love for others; gratitude to God to the service of others. If the motives are wrong, everything else will go wrong. If I do not respect myself, I will respect no one else. There can be no harmony in the community if there is no harmony within people. Internal conflicts lead to external conflicts. If there are flaws in the one, there will inevitably be flaws in the other. The two are bound up and must be dealt with or 'developed' as a whole.

But, fifth, many of the case studies say quite definitely that inner, spiritual transformation is not only a necessity without which development cannot succeed, it is a prior necessity. It must come first. Without it there is little point in going further. First must come purity of motive, since only unselfish, detached development work will ever be regenerating. Otherwise everything goes wrong. 'If you don't change yourself it is not possible to change the world.' First must come the awakening and awareness of the divine and of suffering and its causes. This inner transformation is seen to be the key which unlocks everything else.

Let me finish here with two quotations which not only insist that any holistic view of development must include the spiritual dimension but also hint at the priority of spirituality as inner transformation over everything else:

> While 'development workers' of international agencies view religion and spiritual awakening as irrelevant or even a hindrance to the development process ... experience ... clearly shows how significant spiritual awakening is to development ... development in Western industrialised societies has been measured in terms of GNP, growth rates, per capita income etc. Whereas (in Sarvodaya and other spiritual organizations) development is primarily concerned with one's 'awakening' and inner growth ...[5]

> Instead of social development we talk of self-development and instead of material development, spiritual development, instead of outer development, inner development and instead of uni-dimensional development we have an integrated universal approach.[6]

[5] Case study 10, <www.wfdd.org.uk>, p. 6 (March 2004).
[6] Workshop summary notes, <www.wfdd.org.uk>, p. 11 (March 2004).

The contrast with mainstream Western development and many of its agencies is hardly surprising since they are not faith-based. But the contrast is also with faith-based NGOs in the West (such as Christian Aid) and with my own approach, especially the insistence on the prime importance of inner spiritual transformation as the spring from which all else flows.

Outward and inward

On reflection – and we are talking about 'radical participation' to enrich critical reflection on practice – I realize that my own faith-based approach to development has been concerned more with the outward than the inward. It has drawn on religious teaching – Christian doctrine, worship and ethics – to inform and motivate its policy and practice (and in that sense has had a spiritual dimension) but is has not concerned itself much, if at all, with inner transformation (and in that sense has lacked a spiritual dimension).

A concern with the 'outward' might be characterized in several ways, two of which are obvious. First, it is concerned with structural changes, such as the racist structures of apartheid and, still, our relations with many poor countries, or with reforms of the economic order, including debt cancellation and fairer trading rules. The same concern can be seen in attempts to shift the emphasis of development from aid and charity to advocating for justice and human rights. The second characteristic of an outward approach is a concern with issues of power. If the most telling difference between the rich and the poor, apart from material possessions, is the power they have or don't have to protect themselves and pursue their interests, then the road to justice involves changes to the outward structures of power so that it is counterbalanced and one set of interests cannot easily override another as, for example, is the case in the IFIs and in non-participatory social structures, small and large, of the present day, including so-called democratic structures.

If this concern with the 'outward' has been a reaction to other approaches, either consciously or unconsciously, I suggest it could have been for one or all of the following reasons. First is a general, I don't say justified, unease with overtly religious and spiritual matters in what I have experienced as a secular context. It has often made me glad to pursue the familiar line that arguments based on religious premises, like the Christian faith, do not usually result in overtly religious policy conclusions or in ones that could not be reached or shared by those arguing from non-religious perspectives.

Second is an intellectual distaste for mainstream Western Christianity as it has taken shape over a very long period of its history. In contrast to, say, liberation theology (which also, of course, has its problems) it has generally seen Christian faith as a private, personal and inward matter, settled between a person and their God, and leading to few social responsibilities beyond personal ethical uprightness and acts of charity. Focusing on sin, repentance, conversion and forgiveness as the inner changes that need to come about by faith, it has provided a successful way for the powerful to be religious and maintain a status quo which favours them.

Third, my concern with the outward has been an impatient reaction to the slow-burning fuse of the inward. If social change is to come about, as many Christians still argue, by changing individuals, it is an extremely slow and labour-intensive process, likely to succeed with only a comparative few in my lifetime and even then, like recruiting people to mailing lists and donor databases, likely to lose as many as it gains. This moral and spiritual trickle-down effect is hardly good enough for the millions of marginalized and disadvantaged peoples who look and wait for a reasonable chance to earn a decent living. Outward and structural changes, on the other hand, promise to benefit far more people far more speedily if only we can bring them about. Debt cancellation can save the lives of thousands of children every day by enabling the provision of basic healthcare. Reforming the trade rules can add $100 billion every eight weeks to the incomes of poor countries, opening up possibilities for jobs, schools and hospitals.

Fourth, I have long distrusted being over-fastidious with regard to motives and any suggestion that, if they are not pure and right, then no good can come of them. Motives are usually mixed. People agree on the same actions for different reasons. Varied self-interests may find productive meeting points. Good things may be done for bad reasons. Better to build alliances and get things done whatever the motives than wait for the necessary change of heart and get little or nothing done at all.

Fifth, the contrast between outward and inward, structural change and inner transformation, is also the contrast between the voluntary and the coercive. Inner transformation must be agreed to and permitted by those who are transformed while structural change contains a strong element of coercion. Countervailing power is coercive. Institutional laws, imposing restraints on Transnational Corporations (TNCs), or on countries that subsidize exports to poor countries, or that require decent prices, wages and working conditions, all have about them a significant element of coercion. They make people and organizations do things where otherwise they would not be willing to do them. That, along with many other elements in this outward approach to poverty reduction and human development, could claim to be 'spiritual' in its own right. It wants to love and serve the neighbour in ways that are effective for the neighbour's good; and it respects the Christian assessment of human nature as creative and generous but also as insecure and self-regarding and unlikely to act justly unless it is coerced into doing so.

I am not, therefore, surprised to find myself making a dismissive comment about being 'sidetracked into the more comfortable territories of debate – about spirituality, for example, or more holistic approaches to life, or neglected cultural issues. These are important, but they can never supplant the fundamental import-ance of finding a way to make the world's economy work'.[7] Again, I fully recognize myself in comments from a book dealing with diplomacy, not development, and called *Faith-based Diplomacy: Trumping Realpolitik*: 'faith-based diplomacy speaks to the heart, mind and spirit of the combatants, not simply to the intellectual or material issues that dominate the practice of realpolitik'. As commonly understood it fails to look at a situation whole. It is 'the practice of power politics based on a tough-minded, realistic view of the political, economic and security factors that dominate any given situation'.[8] It leaves out religious considerations.

The sharply contrasting emphasis on the inward rather than the outward, and the voluntary rather than the coercive, which comes out so clearly in these 11 case studies can sound almost regressive to someone who for years has kicked against an evangelistic,

---

[7] Peter Heslam (ed.), *Globalization and the Good* (London: SPCK, 2004), p. 107.

[8] Douglas Johnston (ed.), *Faith-based Diplomacy: Trumping Realpolitik* (New York: Oxford University Press, 2003), pp. x–xi.

pietistic Christian tradition where, for example, conversion can be the be-all and end-all of everything.

Four remarks before I move on.

1. I was challenged and impressed by the case studies for a number of reasons but not least because their spirituality was in no way an alternative to outward structural change in favour of the poor. Every one of the faith communities described was involved in it in one way or another. And although some of the language of 'priorities', and what must come first, and what is 'key' to everything else, has a chronological flavour about it, the main concern is with complementarity: that outward and inward must go together; that one cannot be addressed without the other; that they are mutually influential and interdependent, not discrete; that as a matter of fact neither of them is an instant achievement but progressive and developmental in itself. What matters above all is a holistic approach which includes the spiritual and is thoroughly 'integrated'.

2. A second remark deserves a chapter in itself. It concerns an issue mentioned in the case studies and much discussed in the West as well where, on reflection, we can recognize this 'interrelatedness' or 'integrity' of the outward and the inward and the need to address them both. We do not have to be entirely against the present economic order to recognize its inherent problems, one of which relates to growth. Economic growth is said to be essential for poverty reduction, and in some countries it is. Growth requires not only increasing levels of production and profits for investment, it also requires higher and higher levels of consumption (the British economy has been kept going, according to some commentators, by shoppers). The fear is that growth of this order is not sustainable and can put a burden on our resources and the environment that will lead to a catastrophe even greater than the present poverty of millions. Part of the answer, in so far as we have one, is structural, like reviving the proposal, put forward by Keynes (but rejected) at the time of Bretton Woods, to establish an IFI which would regulate not international debt but international profit, penalizing and levelling out overproduction and disparities between countries and so fostering distribution and sustainability. But if part of the answer is outward, a large part of it is also inward and spiritual. It is not a puritanical attack on enjoying material things, and it should not be a dog-in-the-manger attitude which denies to the have-nots what the haves

have enjoyed for some time. It is a matter of inner transformation, explicitly addressed in the case studies, away from a consumerism which only creates a sense of poverty and a craving for more out of the dissatisfaction it brings in its wake. It is a matter of inner transformation towards a greater degree of detachment and contentment and an awareness of what our human needs really are and how they are met. The outward and inward here are integrally related. The economy needs the consumer if it is to grow, and the consumer pushes the economy towards unsustainable growth. The one is dependent on the other. Both need to change. Development has to be holistic or, better still, 'integrated', including the spiritual with its insistence on inner transformation.

3. A third remark is only to acknowledge that this more integrated approach to development is reflected in writings outside the case studies, some from the pen of Western thinkers. Amartya Sen (careful to avoid a religious label) and, from the Christian tradition, Walter Wink and Mary Grey, would be among them. In the diplomatic sphere I have already referred to *Faith-based Diplomacy: Trumping Realpolitik*, edited by Douglas Johnston.

4. A fourth remark concerns 'Christian social ethics' as I have known it, or maybe now: 'public theology'. The very name suggests a concern with social and structural issues; with the outward rather than the inward; with the public rather than the private. A cursory glance at the evidence, such as the concerns of the very welcome newly created Manchester Centre for Public Theology in the UK, and the essays in *Public Theology for the 21st Century* in honour of Duncan Forester,[9] suggest this may not be far from the truth. And both disciplines, Christian social ethics and public theology, have yet to take much account of the religious plurality of our world today. My question, and it can be no more, is whether the challenge to a more holistic and integrated approach embracing spirituality (which would have nothing to do with theology trying to rule the roost again or reneging on respect for autonomous disciplines) should be addressed to the wider endeavours of Christian social ethics and public theology, not just to development policy and practice.

---

[9] William F. Storrar and Andrew R. Morton (eds.), *Public Theology for the 21st Century* (London: T&T Clark, 2004).

Contrast: sacred places

I turn to the second contrast thrown up by the encounter in New Delhi.

If 'inner transformation' is a necessary element in the whole development process, it raises the obvious question as to how to bring it about. How comes the awakening? How come the changes in awareness of the divine and of self? What can bring about purity of intent, inner quietude or contentment? What ends craving rather than satisfies it? How are different values adopted? One of the answers, in line with an 'integrated' approach, has already been mentioned. It is a chicken-and-egg situation. Inner transformation may open people up to development activities but, equally, involving them in development activities may well promote inner transformation: 'We build the road, the road builds us.' Other answers to the 'how' question, like 'moral education' and 'socialization' are well known. Yet others, like 'meditation', much emphasized by Buddhists, are stranger to many and extremely problematic. It is here, however, that the second striking contrast to emerge from the case studies comes into view.

The communities they describe have a striking attachment to their temples, mosques and churches, which we might refer to generically as 'sacred places'. They all go to them and quite a few are busy building them, like the Swaminarayans in Akshardan and Neasden. They regard them as focal centres for their work on development and link to them a range of activities including worship and ritual, pastoral care, charitable services, spiritual formation, education and training, income-generating projects, social and political action. One senses vibrant life. One dissentient voice in the case studies questions the relevance of temples to development, but everywhere else it is assumed or overtly affirmed.

Now the last thing that mainstream Western development would think of doing (including Christian Aid, though maybe not Tearfund) would be to build a church or mosque or temple or, as I have called them, 'sacred places', out of a conviction that they play a key role in development. There could be political or pragmatic reasons for doing so but otherwise they would be regarded as a distraction. Faith-based development agencies building churches, unable to distinguish between proselytism and spirituality, would be afraid of being mistaken for missionary agencies. Recent research has shown that faith-based agencies tend to be dismissive of the role that local churches can play, leaving them feeling bypassed and underestimated and under-resourced.[10]

It is interesting to note that when Ted Wickham came to make his proposals for a more effective engagement with industrial society, he was critical of local churches (or sacred places) but not dismissive of them. Of his three major suggestions, one was about theology, one was about the structures of industrial mission, and one was about the local church where he advocated the adoption of the Methodist class system in Anglican parishes as a more promising method of formation.[11]

When it comes to wondering what to make of this emphasis on sacred places in the case studies, apart from ignoring it, I can offer no more than a tentative footnote. Setting aside any consider-ations of its implications for faith communities in the South, does it represent any kind of useful challenge to our local church communities here in the North? I have five concluding comments to make.

First, the situation may be so different from Asia that the point has little relevance. Our society is too secular for sacred places like churches to have much influence. Religious teachings carry little weight and, in an age of disintegration, religion does not have a natural place in life (as in India, for example) or easily assume a role. Again, society is too fragmented, even more so than in Wickham's day, for churches to be centres of community. What should not be lost, however, is the urgent need to tackle these two issues: the reintegration of the secular with the spiritual if the advice of the case studies is anything to go by, and the rebirth of community and a sense of belonging.

Second, there are interesting examples of sacred places in our own cities which are highly reminiscent of those in the case studies. Sikh gurdwaras are a good example: vibrant centres of community life with a whole range of activities from spiritual and cultural to political, all of them strengthening and developing their communities in a holistic way. Again, the context may be too different to be relevant. Sikh people are already bound together

---

[10] Taylor, *Christianity, Poverty and Wealth.*
[11] Wickham, *Church and People in an Industrial City,* Ch. 6.

by a common faith and share a sense of exile where establishing and maintaining their identity becomes particularly important.

Third, progressive Christian thinking in recent times, which stresses our responsibility to society, has tended to argue for a minimalist local church. People attend its rituals to find reassurance and renewal and to recover their perspective and a sense of direction, but for little else. The lay movement supported this approach. Lay people were of more use to God and the community outside the church working out their obedience on the 'frontiers' of everyday life. The local church should applaud their absence for most of the time, not require their presence. Salt, as they used to say, is no good in the salt cellar. Arguments about structures and ministry of a generation ago, about mission outside the local church in the workplaces of the world, serviced by non-stipendiaries and worker priests, all ran in the same direction. The rather elaborate picture painted by the case studies of sacred places and how they should function is a far cry from a church that is thought to be better dispersed more often than it is gathered.

Fourth, local churches today may, however, be left with the worst of all worlds. Most of the talk about secular structures for mission (including industrial mission) and secular ministries have faded away and all we have is a minimalist local church, not for sinewy theological or ideological reasons but for all the reasons that John Atherton and others have written about.[12]

Fifth, the case studies with their affirmation of sacred places might offer us food for thought as we reflect critically on the life of our local churches and along the following lines.

1 To begin with, do they suggest a model for its life? It would definitely not be the minimalist model of what I regard as the progressive past. But neither would it be a model for survival, as if the future of the Church as such is the most important consideration, winning its way back into general favour. And it would not be a model for evangelistic activity, recruiting converts to the Christian faith. It is rather a model about development: sacred places as paradigms and agents of holistic development. It understands that the ultimate concern of the local church, in paying due honour to its God, is to work for the common good by

---

[12] See, for example, John Atherton, *Marginalisation* (London: SCM Press, 2003).

helping to develop inclusive, cohesive and outward-looking human communities.

2 If local churches are to think of themselves as agents of development then, according to the case studies, they will adopt a holistic or integrated approach. That will certainly mean promoting and supporting development in all aspects of our life together: political, economic, cultural, social and spiritual. But it could also mean a growing range of imaginative activities of its own, embodying the holism it seeks to promote where cultural and political activities, worship and spirituality are juxtaposed and interrelated, so that the reintegration of our fractured lives is not just an ideal that is preached but a reality that begins to be demonstrated. The 'floating temples' of the Swadhyayans come to mind.

3. Such holistic centres would, of course, have no pretensions to self-sufficiency. They are not in that sense the key to development. Engagement with outward and structural issues of economic and social justice, for example, would continue to require strong partnerships with other agencies and actors, most of them secular or of mixed faith communities, whose contributions are held by the Church, if not by its partners, within an integrated, holistic understanding.

4. Finally, what of inner transformation as a necessary part of the whole? It will come about through involvement in this whole range of integrated developmental activities, including campaigns for justice, cultural expression, prayer and liturgy. Once again, 'The road builds us'. It will be fostered unselfconsciously by such means as spiritual formation, role models and socialization. Where it is taught, it will avoid the spiritualities of privatized religion, of a religion of success, of unattractive moralism or unproductive self-denial. It will constantly affirm a vision of life that is generous, demanding, contented, simple, interesting, enjoyable and satisfying.

All these are matters for further reflection. The challenging question from the case studies, however, remains: what might it mean for a local church, as sacred place, to be a paradigm and agent of holistic development, fostering a 'political' discipleship which reshapes the polis or 'city' where we live for the sake of the common good?

Conclusion

I began this chapter with a question asked by Ted Wickham many years ago. He asked it of the Church in an industrial society. I am asking it mainly of mainstream Western development in the poor world of the South but also, rather tentatively, of the Church and the impoverished communities of the richer world: why have we not been more successful even where we may not have entirely failed? I have described a limited exercise in 'radical participation' in order to nourish critical reflection on our practice. It involved listening to communities from very different contexts and of different faiths. They rather forcefully suggested that our lack of success may be due in part to the fact that, although we have paid lip-service to 'holism', we have not taken it seriously and have failed above all to pay attention to the spiritual as against the material, to the inward as against the outward, to the voluntary as against the coercive, to inner transformation as against structural change, and to recognizing the interrelatedness or 'integrity' of them all. It is not a matter of either–or, however, or of exchanging one emphasis for another. It is a matter of complementarity and of marrying the two.

King Mohosoth and Princess Amara of the title of this chapter feature in a saying found in an old Buddhist text from the Khmer tradition in Cambodia. The text is quoted in one of the case studies[13] in favour of the necessary complementarity of women and men. But it can also remind us in its wry way of the necessary complementarity between Western, mainstream approaches and the more gentle, spiritual approaches of these communities of the South if development is to succeed in promoting the common good. The saying goes like this: 'King Mohosoth is very intelligent, but without tactics (practical common sense?) from Princess Amara – His Majesty is useless'.

---

[13] Case study 11, <www.wfdd.org.uk>, p. 6 (March 2004).

Index